MW00789425

www.redjade.ca



Printed in partnership with Lulu.com Self Publishing.

First Printing, 2019

ISBN 978-0-9939634-4-5

Edited, compiled, and designed by

Red Jade Martial Arts
10525 Jasper Ave
Edmonton, AB, T5J 1Z4

www.redjade.ca

1 3 5 7 9 8 6 4 2

# Secrets of Drunken Boxing
## In the Eight Shadow Style

## Volume 3
## Internal Alchemy

by SIfu Neil Ripski

# Preface

Although this book's title is Secrets of Drunken Boxing, it is much more than that. The internal training, alchemy, and Nei Gong contained within comes not just from my experience with the Ma Family Drunken. They are compiled from many different sources to help the student progress from external training to internal. To have strong Drunken style martial arts, a great deal of internal training must be understood and done appropriately. High-level martial arts rely heavily on the taming of the mind, cultivation of the internal, and application of the art to oneself as well as others. Before the drunken boxer can begin to enter the advanced levels of training in dealing with the immortals and more esoteric Qigong training, a sturdy foundation must be laid in the internal training itself.

Throughout this book, I have compiled information on internal training from Drunken Style Internal Alchemy, Ma Family Style Qigong, 18 Lohan Palm Qigong, Shaolin Traditional Qigong training, and more. My own understanding and progression in the internal arts is a result of the thirty years of cross-referencing and integration of practice under various traditions. I aim to pass on some depth as well as a breadth of knowledge in this book. I hope it helps in the long run of your training, for your martial arts are your own, and no one else's.

# Drunken Boxing & Internal Training

Drunken boxing is typically looked at as an advanced method of training and taught late in the curriculum of other styles. Generally, this is due to the physical requirements of the drunken forms which need some strong Gongfu from previous training. But this is only the surface level of understanding of Drunken. Not only is it a mental switch from orthodox to unorthodox methods of fighting and movement but it is a system of training that is meant to shift the perspective of the student from outside to inside, from physical ability to internal ability, from the beginner levels of martial training to the advanced. Without the cultivation of the internal, the Drunken boxer remains only a shell of techniques and forms with little depth.

The term Internal can have many meanings and to the martial artist it is a mystical term that is rarely ever defined. Internal training has many parts for the Drunken player or any martial artist in general. It includes training and taming the mind and its parts (Yi Intellect, Xin Heart or Emotions, Shen Spirit), understanding the difference between Pre- and Post-heaven parts of themselves, what internal power is, understanding and cultivating Dantian and its six directions, and more. Looking inwards to understand the outward part of martial arts training leaves us looking directly into ourselves, not only our ability but who we are as martial artists. The higher level you want to attain in martial arts, the more you must train in a balanced way. External or internal can only get half way. and the other is needed to make one's training whole.

What follows is my attempt at breaking down and presenting how I teach students internal when they become ready. It is meant as a guide to bring someone forward from beginner to intermediate levels of training. Taken carefully into a student's personal routine and training I have seen excellent results, and they pass through intermediate stages in time. Advanced martial arts, and Drunken Boxing in particular, is something that needs to be prepared for and not rushed into. I hope this helps.

by Sifu Neil Ripski

# Qigong Training Foundations

To train Qigong thoroughly and to gain the expected results it is essential to have strong foundations. Many Qigong books I have read over the years detail training of various intermediate to high-level practices without any firm grounding in foundational concepts of what Qi is, the philosophy Qigong is rooted in, or explanations of esoteric concepts like Dantian and so on. Although this book started as an article on training methods, it quickly grew into a document meant to help preserve the various Qigong I have been privileged enough to learn and train over the past thirty years. I hope that the foundations here will be explained adequately to avoid mistakes in training later down the road.

## The Concept of Qi (氣)

Qi is the most hotly debated topic in not only Qigong practices but internal martial arts and indeed martial arts in general. Without an understanding of how to approach the concept of Qi, it is easy to try and just guess what the sensations and methods are meant to accomplish.

Many people go on and on about 'Cultivating your Qi' 'Building Qi' and 'Refining the Qi'. In some esoteric literature from past Qigong masters, we find flowery language trying to describe internal feelings and movements that involve complex body mechanics to arrive at seemingly mystical results.

Even today we see many Qigong and martial arts masters able to perform feats that seem superhuman and when asked how they simply respond 'Qi'.

This answer is correct, but it is of little use to the person who is trying to train and cultivate their own Qi. This usually ends up being the cycle of a Qigong taught to them by their master and repeated throughout their lives in the blind faith that something magical will happen. In some cases, the training does work, and they become able to perform feats like their own teachers. Unfortunately, the flaw in this method, in my opinion, is that it ends up with the same answer. The teachers really cannot describe what they are doing and can only teach it in the same way they learned it; without any understanding or careful guidance.

If we look at the Chinese character for Qi, 氣, we can see three parts to it. A fire pictured under a pot and steam rising from that pot. This is where the translation of Qi as life energy comes from. Although that is a correct term to use it is still obscure. And when we are trying to retrain ourselves through these methods, obscurity is not our friend. Why is it translated as life energy? Well if you were in China in ancient times and a pot was on to boil, you were most likely making food, which meant life itself. Eating every day was not a standard luxury in China in the past and being able to eat meant you could continue to live. But the term Qi is more than that. If you picture yourself entering your home and seeing the pot on to boil and smell the delicious scent of, say Chicken Noodle Soup, you might be reminded of being cared for by your mother when you were young and sick, or maybe a cold winter's day when you sat by the fire and drank soup with loved ones. It is not just the sustenance implied by the word Qi but the relationship you have with that pot of water. It is also the smell, the memories of your mother, memories of warmth, of eating nourishing food, your relationships to the entire set.

As my Gongfu brother Professor Kevin Wallbridge says, Qi is best defined by the English word relationship. This allows it to imply so much more than a single thing and will enable us to look closely at what relationships an exercise is working on. So, we can look now at common phrases used in the community such as cultivating Qi as building and strengthening relationships, perhaps relationships between body and mind, different joints, different muscular chains, or in the cases of some more transformative Qigong, your relationship with reality.

Using the word relationship makes so much of the obscurity in Qigong training disappear that it is worthwhile to study any reference to Qi with this is mind. Building powerful relationships in your body is the result of long-term training and is the way Masters perform their seemingly magical feats. This allows students learning Qigong to ask the right questions and not just repeat motions over and over hoping for results. What relationship are you working? In what way?

## A Brief Summary of Yin and Yang

The concept of Yin and Yang is often misunderstood in martial arts or understood only on a rudimentary level. Traditional Chinese Medicine training goes into some depth when looking at this Taoist method of thought to use it for the basis of diagnostics later in training. Martial Artists tend to go into less depth than doctors in training but know the basic concept of Yin and Yang can play a significant role in understanding more difficult aspects of Chinese thought and Internal practice and it is well worth investigating even more deeply than discussed here.

The Taiji Diagram, or as many call it in English, the Yin Yang. is a model of the universe itself. To define and discuss any one thing, we must imply or outright define its opposite. If we want to discuss aspects of any one thing the use of Yin and Yang as ideas are always present. The misconceptions most familiar to the discussion of Taiji theory are what I will attempt to address briefly.

Taiji, usually translated as The Grand Ultimate, is often misunderstood, especially in the context of martial arts as a grand ultimate or 'best' style Tai Ji Quan. The translation is correct, but it leaves room for some discussion as to the second character, Ultimate. The Character Ji can be more deeply translated as a point of transformation between Yin and Yang. For example, if an object is thrown in the air, there is a moment when the upwards movement stops and transforms to downwards movement. It is this moment that is the Ji or ultimate point of transformation between Yin and Yang. In practice of the internal martial arts, it is a subject of in-depth study in movement and stillness, looking to where one ends and the other begins.

But Yin and Yang theory demands that there always be a context. There is nothing that is simply yang or yin, there must be a relationship, a context in which it is being discussed. It is like two sides of a coin - one yin, one yang, one coin. There cannot be only one side to the coin to discuss. Therefore, there is always context.

Examples of Yin and Yang are classically given in medical textbooks, and most martial artists have been exposed to them. Classically Yang things are Heaven, Fire, Up, Light, Sun, Male, and so on. This, of course, means that Yin things are: Earth, Water, Darkness, Moon, Female, and such. These classic examples are used to create the context for the person studying so that they can understand and define things themselves. If Yang aspects are Heaven (ethereal), Fire (hot, burning, outward, upward) and Yin aspects the opposite to them, we can see that it becomes a simple example of the context to define something.

Nothing is strictly Yin or Yang. Only in relationship to something else can they be defined. This is the most crucial aspect of the concept for the martial artist.

Regarding martial usage, we can see how a Yang attack is met with a Yin defense to create balance and harmony between you and the opponent. To meet force with force is double heavy and relies on superior strength rather than higher understanding and skill, and it cannot be relied on. There is always someone faster or stronger, more yang, than we are.

Regarding internal training, it is essential to understand the idea of Yin and Yang to balance one's practice. Pure external training is unbalanced, as is only internally thinking. A great mind housed in a poorly trained body is disconnected and weak and of no use to the martial artist. On a deeper internal level of training understanding the balance of heat and cooling, Yang and Yin Qigong practices are vital to maintaining stability and health. Without the balance of the mental and physical, the real and imagined, there is a chance of training incorrectly and suffering not only from stunted progress but Qigong sickness and real ailments. I recommend studying this more than I have gone here by looking at the Yin side of martial arts Traditional Chinese Medicine - and reading more deeply about the subject.

# Origin of Dantian (丹田)

Dantian (丹田) is always referred to as the place a few finger-widths below the navel and inside the body. This is behind the acupoint known as Qi Hai (氣海) or, The Sea of Qi, and this point is often mistaken as Dantian itself. In Qigong and martial arts training lower Dantian, which we are discussing, is used as a metaphor not only for the centre of the body itself but as an origin point of the movement. For example, in Drunken Style, we use the image of a half-full wine gourd centred here that moves and sloshes the wine before the external body is moved.

In Qigong practices and most martial arts, Dantian is described as a sphere at this point in the body where the origin of movement begins and where the Qi resides. This concept and its source are an excellent place to start understanding Dantian and Qigong practices in general.

If we go look far enough back into ancient history, we find the tribal people of the world, in this case China, looking for answers. The world around them is unknown and unexplained and it is from this state they begin trying to understand and describe things to themselves. It is this process that gave us the ideas of spirits in rivers and forests, gods pulling the sun across the sky, and so on. When it came to the human body, another great mystery needed explanation.

Here I will paraphrase a lesson my Gongfu brother Kevin Walbridge uses when teaching the fundamentals of Chinese Medicine and Qigong. A process of thought might begin with the understanding that when a person eats something, they feel good in their centre, or around their navel. They then have the energy to do work and play, which eventually runs out. Hunger begins, and they need to eat again. So logically eating something makes you feel good by your navel and must store energy there, which you can use to live your life. When this energy stored runs out you must fuel up again.

It is this kind of thinking that leads to the idea that Dantian stores energy brought into and processed by the body, called Post-heaven Qi. This is the energy we are working to harness in most Qigong training, or so many people believe. Sometimes, however, the relationship being worked on is something entirely mental such as the relationship between your breath and your stomach. This work continues until it enters strange territory, or alchemical or magical Qigong used for studying relationships outside the self.

# Pre and Post-heaven Qi

There are many different classifications of Qi used in traditional Chinese medicine, Qigong and, martial arts but for the sake of building a foundation from which to work, we need to look first at Pre- and Post-heaven Qi. Plainly these are the Qi from before you see the sky and after you see the sky a poetic description of birth. Pre-heaven Qi is inherited from your parents and cannot be changed through diet or training while Post-heaven Qi is the energy you bring into your body to live by eating, drinking, breathing, and some forms of Qigong. It is important to realize how precious the Pre-heaven Qi is as you only receive a finite amount and it is essentially the stuff of life. When it runs out you die. The following chart was taught to me as a way of understanding the relationships between Pre- and Post-heaven, the three treasures of Jing, Qi, and Shen, and what is referred to as Ling in Qigong and traditional Chinese medicine. The deeper you understand the thought processes and cultural context of how these things were created and what they are based upon, the more deeply your foundations will be built. That, in turn, affects your ability to reach high levels of skill.

## Hun & Po, Shen & Jing, and Ling

Ling (靈) is an interesting character made up of different radicals. The top of the character 雨 is a picture of a rain cloud. Underneath are three mouths pictured as boxes which implies chanting or singing. The bottom of the character has two parts to understand. 人 is the character for a person, and when combined with the dividing lines it creates 巫, the character for Shaman or Witch. So, when all put together, the character 靈 means the essence that the shaman calls upon when he does the rain dance. This is sometimes interpreted as the universe, god, or spirits. However, you translate it, the meaning suggests the universe or spirit world that exists both before and after your life.

I like to think of it like a beach filled with trillions of grains of sand. When a new organism is conceived a spark of Ling, a single grain of sand, is attracted to the new organism, giving it the spark of life, and so we read the chart from the left.

From the left we see Ling meeting a line running horizontally across the page. This is the passage of life from conception on the left to the moment of Birth ][ until it reaches the Ling again on the right of the image where death would occur. The vertical line is the separation between the Pre-heaven and the Post-heaven of a person's life. On the Pre-heaven side we have Hun and Po, and on the Post-heaven side, we see Shen and Jing. The line between them representing life is also describing the relationship between these sets, thus it is Qi.

## Pre-heaven is Hun & Po and Post-heaven is Shen & Jing

Hun and Po (魂 and 魄) literally translate to cloud soul and white soul respectively. There are many references to this soul duality in different Taoist traditions and further back in time there are references to Sanhunqipo (三魂七魄) or the Three Hun and Seven Po. This deals more with the Shamanic traditions of entities that possess or exist within the human being and influence their health and minds.

The discussion of Pre-heaven and Post-heaven are comparable to Yin and Yang. The Shen is the Post-heaven of the Hun and the Jing the Post-heaven version of the Po. With this basis, we can define each of these aspects of ourselves with context.

The Shen can be labelled as one's Acquired Self or a person's self that has interacted with reality, other people, situations, culture, and so on. Shen is translated as Spirit in English but also encompasses one's mind, intellect, and emotional state, because it acts upon and reacts to reality. The Pre-heaven version of the Shen is the Hun. This can be called one's True Self, the person they are before they are born. Each human being has different callings, passions, talents, and innate abilities. Not everyone's Hun is that of a lawyer, for example, or a carpenter. While many people can enter these professions, only a few seem naturally drawn to them. Usually, these people become innovators in their field and genuinely become masters.

## Buddhist Breathing

Buddhist breathing is referred to as belly breathing, diaphragmatic breathing, or sometimes bellows breathing. It comes from the Indian practices that were transferred to China alongside Buddhism. It is the method of inhaling through the nose deeply and allowing the abdomen to expand, then exhaling and letting the belly to contract back to its normal state. It is taught in meditation and Buddhist Qigong methods as a foundational exercise.

Buddhist breathing is considered Post-heaven breathing as it utilizes the idea of Dantian being a storehouse for Post-heaven Qi and that it can be filled with more Qi from eating, drinking and, of course, breathing deeply. The imagery used is that Dantian is like a hollow sphere and each inhalation fills and expands Dantian with new Qi to be refined. It is a relaxing method of breathing that allows the lungs to work efficiently through the length and depth of the breath. Experiments on this type of deep breathing have shown that the body relax and the reduction of stress.

As with most everything in martial or Qigong training, Buddhist breathing methods have different levels. Typically, I do not initially share the following because the basic foundations are the most important in discussions with students. But for this book I thought a little more detail may be appreciated.

Buddhist breathing as discussed above is the foundational method of the practice, with the belly expanding on inhalation. The next level of this breathing is to have the entire Dantian area extend when doing this breathing method. Most people when they start can open the belly and allow it to expand or contract as they breathe but tend only to have it expand forward from the spine. What you want to happen is the belly area extends backwards as well as forwards. This can be taught most easily by having someone place their palms on your lower back near your kidneys. Expanding the belly back into their palms as well as forward seems awkward at first, but with some mind intent helped along by the tactile input of a partner's hands, it can be accomplished relatively quickly.

## Dantian & Six Directions

Dantian should be seen at this stage as having six directions or sides: front, back, left, right, up, and down. Initially, you and cultivates the front wall of Dantian with Buddhist breathing. Working to engage the back of Dantian with a partner is trained next. With a partner then holding their palms on the sides of the body just below the rib cage you can learn to have the left and right sides of Dantian expand as well when breathing. It is important to remember this is not a forced engagement of the muscularity of the torso. It is a result of relaxation, softness, and expanding the Dantian area gently. Too much interstitial pressure can result in all kinds of health issues, which is the reason this is not openly taught most of the time. Relax into the breath and let the body expand as it can with a little awareness from the mind.

To train the top of Dantian, a you or a partner should place a palm just below the solar plexus just below your rib cage and teach your breathing. Dantian should expand forward and slightly upward towards the chest cavity, creating a small shelf on the top of the belly pressing gently upwards. Again, be gentle with this training, using the mind to influence the body rather than forcing it.

The bottom of Dantian is challenging to cultivate as it is rarely discussed and can result in problems if done incorrectly. Specifically, Fox Shen as it is known in Traditional Chinese Medicine (Hernia) is the most common complication. When doing the Buddhist method of training the floor of Dantian is prepared during the exhalation of the breath rather than the inhalation as with all other sides. The bottom of Dantian is not meant to be engaged with much strength and acts like a trampoline Dantian rests upon, a supporting floor with flex and muscular tonus, not hard power.

To train the floor of Dantian when exhaling, place one of your hands on the perineum or Hui Yin located between the anus and genitals. Flex this area gently on exhalation as though you are pulling upwards into the torso; this exercise is also known as Kegels in the west. For men, the genitals should smoothly move upwards towards the body but with no pain or real strength exerted. Gently pull only with the muscles of the torso. This is then released like a pressure valve when the breath changes back to the expanding inhalation.

Now ideally you can train the Buddhist breathing method with all six directions engaged. Be gentle and careful with yourself as you are exercising deep muscularity in ways that can cause hernias, muscle tearing, and blood pressure increases. Gentleness with the mind and the body is vital here.

So why train this way? Being able to expand and contract the torso or Dantian in all these directions has many different benefits.

## Refining the Qi in Dantian

Although I am using the classical language here, we now know that it means refining and exercising the relationships in the muscularity of the torso. Martial artists can gain quite a benefit from this as the more refined the engagement of the torso is when used as an origin point for the movement of the body, the more connected and powerful the movement becomes.

The relationships do not end with the muscularity of the torso and their engagement, however. Breathing in this way and expanding in all directions massages the internal organs and washes them with blood. Most internal organs rely on a certain amount of muscular contraction to push blood through them and when people are sedentary stagnant blood can pool in the organs resulting in less efficient function. This helps organ health and ultimately longevity.

The use of the perineum during exhalation is especially suitable for male practitioners as this action massages the prostate gland which has multiple positive effects on sexual health and erectile function, and positive impact on mental health as well. Emotionally, the lower Dantian is associated with base functions of the body. This is not just speculation from tradition. The Buddhist breathing method in six directions also engages and massages the brachial plexus located in front of the spine. A cluster of nerves like this can be considered an electrical event in the body like the heart and the brain perhaps not so coincidentally the locations of the other two Dantians. These electrical events and their effect on the movement of information through the nervous system has a profound impact on the practitioner including calming the mind and emotions by lowering blood pressure and essentially gently massaging the nervous system. The classical language would say the meridians in the belly are stretched and compressed through this type of breathing, allowing each of them to be affected positively and the flow of Qi to become smooth and unhindered. All the meridians of the body are tied together by Dai Mai, called the belt meridian, which means the entire system is being massaged. The non-duality of the mind and body connection as it is approached in Chinese Medicine is especially relevant here. I recommend that if you want to learn more about the emotions, mind, and body in Chinese Medicine do not just accept the standard level of each organ system and its associated emotions. Research Qing Shi Bing, mental and emotional healing, in Chinese Medicine to get a better idea.

> "To treat the Mind, treat the Body. To treat the Body, treat the Mind."
>
> Traditional Chinese Medicine Axiom.

## Refined & Unrefined Qi in Buddhist Breathing

This is a concept that was passed down through oral tradition to me by Master Ma during my training. The idea of different types or states of Qi is not unknown and can be seen in Traditional Medicine in many ways. For example, Zong Qi (Ancestral), Wei Qi (Outside or guardian Qi), Gu Qi (Nutritive Qi) and so on.

In this tradition, there are different states of Post-heaven Qi that are gained through the practice of breathing exercises and Qigong. Qi that is brought into the body through Buddhist breathing methods to reside in Dantian is from the outside, or fresh Qi. It has not been refined yet by Dantian. Typically, when we need the energy to exercise or concentrate the mind, this Post-heaven

Qi is used as fuel for daily life. Refining this type of Qi is like adding octane to gasoline; it accomplishes the same goals but has a little more power when it does so.

Refining Qi in Dantian is not an exercise but instead a process that some would call internal alchemy. To start from the basic understanding of this line of thinking we must establish a couple of things. First, Dantian is made up of two characters (丹田). The second character is a rice paddy from above, a place where food is grown. The first character, - Dan (丹) - is a picture of a cooker or furnace with a pill or pellet inside it. This is usually translated as the furnace where the pill of immortality is created, and some began translating it as cinnabar, a substance thought to be in the herbal concoction of the pill of immortality. If we look at the idea that the furnace is the place that cooks and transforms the herbs into the magical pill, we can start to understand the concept of refining the Qi in Dantian.

The meaning I am using for this section of Qi is that of energy that can be brought into the body and used, like food has calories or water is needed for regulation and maintenance. In this case, proper breathing brings more Qi into the Dantian than shallow untrained breathing.

So, the refining of the fresh Qi in Dantian is quite simple. If one breathes with the Buddhist method, the Qi is brought directly to Dantian to be stored. The furnace of Dantian is stoked, heated, activated, by the practice of breathing methods, meditation, Qigong, or internal cultivation of any sort. In this way, Buddhist breathing is like making deposits in a bank account. Further training allows for the deposits to continue and the refining of the Qi is like the interest. The more training is done, the more deposited, and the more the interest begins to add up.

Expenditure of this refined Qi comes from poor life and health choices, overwork, stress, or the use of it to fuel other types of internal training. In this way, you can see the foundations become more critical than the high-level methods. Without the fuel to use for the practice, the exercise becomes muddled, inefficient and possibly dangerous, leading to Qigong sicknesses.

So, train the basics more than anything else, and the Qi will become more refined. Do not expend your energy on stupid things like processing crappy food or ideas. Train every day, even a little, and the benefits begin to stack up. Using the refined Qi to accomplish high-level training methods is a powerful and valid way to train, just be sure to have the fuel stored up before undertaking costly training methods.

People tend to ask me then what kinds of methods are costly. Good examples would be things like Vipassana meditation, emptiness meditation trance states, some techniques of Fa Qi (Qi healing), and others. Any training essentially forcing something to happen is dangerous and costly to the person training it. It is worth the risks and building of the foundations in my opinion, but you should always be informed and working to keep safe and healthy.

# Taoist Breathing

Taoist methods are the native methods of thought, philosophy, and training in China. When Buddhism expanded from India, it ran into Taoism and when the smoke cleared Chan (Zen) was born. The Taoist methods are where Qigong and traditional Chinese medicine originated and as such their foundations of breathing are different than the Buddhists lineages and closely follow Chinese Medical theory.

Sometimes referred to as reverse breathing, Taoist breathing methods appear to be the opposite of the Buddhist as the belly contracts during inhalation and expands during exhalation. Unfortunately, this is where the discussion ends for many people and the reasons are never explained. The old method of teaching, where the student does merely as the master says without question, can work but rarely does it result in deep knowledge of the practice.

Dantian is the storehouse for Post-heaven Qi which is gained from eating, drinking, and breathing and as such it can be replenished. Buddhist breathing focuses on expanding and filling Dantian during breathing practice and refining the Qi within. Taoist breathing involves moving Dantian towards Ming-men during the breath cycle and back into place during exhalation.

## The Method

When inhaling, pull your navel backwards and upwards towards your kidneys and spine. As you begin to exhale let the top of the belly release first and then the lower abdomen to finish the breath. In classical language: Inhale and pull Dantian backwards and upwards towards Ming-men, as you begin to exhale Dantian moves forward from Ming-men and then settles down to its original position.

## Ming-men (命门)

Ming-men is a subject that is enormous, deep, and difficult. When I first asked my 18 Lohan Master Chen Qi Ming, A famous Chinese Doctor and Qigong master in southern China, he walked back into his office and returned with a paperback manual about three inches thick, all in Chinese.

"All Ming-men," he told me, "very difficult." So, while my knowledge of Ming-men may be shallow in the grand scheme of things I will do my best to describe it from the perspective of Qigong and Taoist breathing.

Ming-men is roughly located in the area around the kidneys. There is controversy about its exact location where some say it is in the left kidney and others say it is between them. For the purposes of Taoist breathing, it is between the kidneys, near the adrenal glands, and near the spine. It is home to the Pre-heaven or inherited Qi. Pre-heaven Qi cannot be replenished and is the inherited or ancestral (Zong) Qi that is passed down from one's parents. Thus, if parents are healthy, young, live cleanly in a pleasant climate and environment, their offspring tend to be healthy as well. Pre-existing genetic traits like eye colour, skin colour or even genetic disorders that are passed down from generation to generation are considered Pre-heaven (before you are born/see the sky) and cannot be changed.

Pre-heaven Qi is also the magic within the creation of life through conception. Many things are passed on to us through our genetics and therefore stuff like natural life expectancy, predisposition to addiction, etc., are also a part of our Pre-heaven selves. This is sometimes referred to as our Po or corporeal soul, our genetics. The other aspect of our Pre-heaven self is called our Hun, our true selves, our cloud-soul (魂). This is who we are before we interact with the world.

Qigong methods that use Taoist breathing work on the power of Pre-heaven Qi to help with the training-induced transformation. By pulling Dantian to Ming-men during breathing, a tiny amount of the Pre-heaven Qi is temporarily released into the body and can be used to help that transformation or, if the Qigong is done incorrectly, it can even be lost.

Training just Taoist breathing methods should be done until it becomes natural and comfortable before using it during any other Qigong. A Dantian and Ming-men are like flint and steel. Bringing Dantian to Ming-men strikes them together and releases a spark of the Pre-heaven Qi into the body. The Qi will follow the mind (Yi Ling Qi) and as such the mind needs to be still and focused on what is going on during training. Exhaling and bringing Dantian forward and settling it down to its original position allows things to return to their natural state. Returning Qi to Dantian, or merely keeping the mind on Dantian as it relaxes, leads the Qi back to its original state. So, Pre-heaven Qi will return to Ming-men after having been released into the body for a short time.

Consider another metaphor to understand the reason for releasing the Pre-heaven Qi into the body during Qigong training. Every cell in the body is alive thus it is and has Qi. If we think of each cell as a soldier in an army, they must take commands from somewhere to stay organized. Dantian is like this Commanding officer, so when Dantian is active during Qigong, it is like a Colonel giving orders to the troops and inspecting and watching them do their jobs. Ming-men is like the Emperor.

If troops are working and the Colonel comes by to inspect them, they pay attention and do their jobs. But when the Emperor himself comes to inspect the troops they give it their best. They work harder, more efficiently and adequately than ever before. Releasing the Pre-heaven Qi from Ming-men is like having the Emperor personally inspect the progress of the troops in every breath.

Pre-heaven Qi is like an account of reserve energy. It is the stuff that helps create life with a mate and real powerful transformation, but no discussion about it would be complete without talking about how we expend it ourselves as well.

When we are young and have an older brother or friend bootleg alcohol for them, the drunken party ensues, and in the morning the young person wakes up with little to no hangover. From the perspective of Ming-men this happens. The Liver comes to Ming-men and says, “We have been poisoned!” but Ming-men, who is the keeper of this reserve account of Pre-heaven Qi looks and sees a large balance. Ming-men then gives a grain of the Pre-heaven to the liver to help it filters the poison out efficiently, spending that grain of Pre-heaven to do it. No hangover.

Time and time again this happen as the person starts to enjoy alcohol and of course the pleasure is met with little to no pain as Ming-men keeps helping the liver out with some Pre-heaven Qi each time. But one day Liver comes to Ming-men and asks for help with, yet another round of poisoning and Ming-men sees the balance in the account is only big enough to handle day to day endeavours for the rest of this person's life and refuses to let liver have any Pre-heaven Qi. That morning the person gets the mother of all hangovers as the liver is trying to do all the work it can but has no help.

The most poignant phrase my Gongfu brother Kevin said to me about this subject, "What you spend in your 20s, you pay for in your 60s."

As Ming-men becomes weaker and has less Pre-heaven Qi to spare because it is being used just to keep your body functioning. Then, what will be the quality of your life? Excess Pre-heaven means a spry, powerful person even at advanced age, but someone who spent their excess Pre-heaven early in life will have health troubles, reduced quality of life, and will pay the price for spending it all. Of course, the choice is ours to make but as Qigong practitioners and martial artists, we should be aware that Pre-heaven Qi cannot be regained or rebuilt. It is a finite amount, and when it runs out, we perish. Be careful what you chose to use it on.

Finally, another way of looking at Ming-men is referenced a great deal in traditional Chinese medicine as Ming-men Fire. This way of seeing it is like the fire of life itself, the power reserve that keeps the body going and running. There is much more to it than this, beyond my own understanding, but I am sure you get the idea. It is like the glue that keeps the spirit anchored in the body, the Yang pinned to the Yin of the flesh. When that fire goes out, the glue lets go and Yin and Yang separate. The Spirit (Hun) returns to the Ling, and the Flesh (Jing) returns to the Earth.

The point I am trying to drive home here is that Taoist breathing is quite potent and should be taken seriously in training. It is not dangerous to train. Just practice the breathing until it can be done without a lot of direction by the mind on the physical apparatus of the breath. Then move into using it in Qigong. Most Qigong are safe and are not going to harm the practitioner's Pre-heaven Qi at all. But this is why information is essential when it comes to Qigong training and why every Qigong book says you should train with a real teacher for safety's sake.

There are literally whole books of information written about Ming-men and its functions in the body. I am by no means a great expert in it, so please be aware any mistakes or omissions are merely my own.

# Observations about Buddhist & Taoist Breathing in Training

Having trained both types of breathing during meditation and Qigong since beginning my martial arts life in 1986, I experimented and asked many questions of my teachers and myself as to the uses of the different methods. I had mixed results in different practices with these two methods of breathing but will attempt to sum up what I have experienced.

My student and disciple David Mannes of New York, who has a deep interest and background in healing arts that involve the use of breath, had a great thought about these two methods. Buddhist breathing activates the nervous system in a way that removes external phenomena and allows for relaxation and contemplation. Taoist breathing enables the nervous system in a more exciting way that prepares one for movement, fight or flight reactions, and hunting or chasing prey.

While it seems like the two methods can be used interchangeably in Qigong, my experience mirrors his thoughts about the nervous system. Meditation, contemplation, and relaxation practices seem to be best served with Buddhist breathing and its qualities of settling and releasing. Qigong practices that are active either outwardly with movement or inwardly with innervation seem best supported with Taoist breathing methods. For example, Taoist breathing would be used for Qigong like the Shaolin Internal Iron-Palm system of Heavy Hands. The body remains static in posture while the mind activates the nervous system as though the action is about to take place.

When it comes to meditation or seated practices that resemble meditation, the type of breathing used depends a great deal on the actual internal working and the effect you are trying to create. For example, meditation on a fundamental level is the release of the mind's scattered thoughts. It brings the ten thousand things we think about down to two or one or even none, just sitting. Buddhist style meditation like this is about the release and letting go of thoughts and is best served with Buddhist style breathing. The release of the abdomen (Dantian) and relaxation of the torso and its many nerve plexus tends to create a feeling of wellbeing, relaxation, and letting go which is ideal for mediation training. In many cases, the less the body interferes with the mind and its letting go of various thoughts the more efficiently a state of one-pointedness can come for the practitioner.

However, active seated meditation Qigong training or Nei Gong work like Five Hearts Qigong from the Ma family creates a state of readiness or dynamic change in the mind and body perception. This activeness can be supported nicely with Taoist breath work. In the case of something like Eagle Claw Gong, the mind is in a state of telling the fingers to reach and stretch to the walls, open the joints of the wrists, elbows, and shoulders constantly. While this is almost entirely a mental exercise, it is active, and the constant reaching is much like the preparation to leap upon prey, so the more active Taoist method is useful here.

Of course, these are just my observations. While I may have been training longer than some, the only way to really know what works best for you in your training is to experiment with both. Pay attention to the warnings about incorrect practice and how to detect and avoid it. I have made many mistakes as I was always that person who tests the warnings to see if they are folktales or real worries. Most of the old writings and warnings about Qigong appear to be true. Proceed wisely but with the wonder of a child looking to experience things for the first time. Expect nothing, observe everything!

## Warnings & Rules for Qigong Practice

These are old rules from Qigong teachers that have been passed down through generations. Some, I have personally tested and seen their validity and others appear to be more folk-tale than teachings. I leave them here for you to decide.

Do not practice Qigong directly after eating
Do not practice Qigong while hungry
Do not practice Qigong in the Wind or Cold
Do not practice Qigong in a rainstorm
Do not practice Qigong when there is a thunderstorm
Do not practice Qigong when exhausted

Practice Qigong before eating or one hour after
Practice Qigong in comfortable surroundings
Practice Qigong in appropriate clothing
Practice is best in the morning at sunrise, facing south
Practice is best done on the same day each day

Some personal advice from my own practices:

Qigong practice should not make the bones hot, fix this in your mind "The bones are light and cool while the flesh is heavy and wet."

Pay no more attention to heat or visions than you would to a passing dog. See it and let it go.

Observe, do not create sensations.

# Taoist Alchemy & Immortality

by Sifu Neil Ripski

The following information was passed to me by my Shifu Chen Qi Ming while teaching me 18 Lohan Palm. Shifu (Dr.) Chen is a famous Chinese Doctor from Guangzhou China and his specialty in his later years has been the study of longevity and Taoist Immortality. He began his training in Qigong methods during his youth and has continued throughout his life with an interest in longevity. He is currently dividing his time between Edmonton, Alberta, Canada where both of his daughters run his Herbal and Acupuncture clinic and Guangzhou where he treats patients and teaches medicine and Qigong at the university.

This information was passed to me using a diagram to make the complicated terms and methods clear and to show the progression of training and its results. It's like having a roadmap. Being able to see the mountain across the valley and deciding to climb it is good, but it is a lot easier with a map of the trails that lead to the summit. Either way will work, but one is a lot easier and more likely to succeed.

The diagram is built based on Jing Qi Shen transformation and so we must understand these terms and how they apply to the process.

## The Diagram of Filling Three Basins

To understand what this is mapping out, we need to look first at the Yin and Yang continuum on the left side of the diagram. The bottom of the diagram is considered Yin which in this case implies negative or drawing in. In my teacher's, words Negative Qi is the Realm of Hungry Ghosts and Demons. Entities that have lived can become wandering Hungry Ghosts. Those that have never lived but are negative, in the sense of parasitic relationships with the living, are known as Demons. Both Hungry Ghosts and Demons attach themselves to living beings to survive by sucking life energy (Qi) from them. My teacher referred to this realm as negative Qi or the realm of the dead.

Moving towards the top of the diagram, the first double line separates the living from the dead. The top is considered Yang and is the Realm of Immortals and Buddhas. The Yang end of this spectrum refers to it as Positive, ethereal, and self-sufficient in relationship to the Yin Realm of Hungry Ghosts and Demons. Immortals and Buddhas do not need to gather energy from other sources to remain. Their attainment is so high that not only do they self-sustain but have an enormous excess of energy (Qi).

In between these two extremes, we have the world of the living. The world of cultivation and the people who train and cultivate is divided into two parts, more Yin or Yang. From the double line at the bottom to the dividing line in the middle, you have the realm of normal human life as Master Chen said. The lower double line represents death and the separation of the body (Yin) from the spirit/Shen (Yang). The upper line represents normal human maximum and refers to a level of health and cultivation that is rare.

Within the first level of cultivation towards normal human maximum we see three separate basins or frameworks of cultivation practice called Jing Xue, Qi Xue, and Shen Xue. These are the three treasures of Jing, Qi, and Shen referred to in many different Chinese cultivation methods, and the addition of Xue (Blood) means it is the Jing, Qi, or Shen that is rooted in the body as a part of the typical human experience. Each of these is like a basin or bowl that we need to fill through practice to come closer and closer to the normal human maximum. A person that reaches the line of human maximum would have all three of these basins filled from practice. Each basin can fill through cultivation on its own and if filled will begin to trickle over the edges into another basin. This explains how a cultivator with years and years of only meditative practices can still fill the Qi and Jing Basins through constant proper training.

To understand this better we need to define the three treasures and what they represent for the cultivator. Jing is sometimes translated as essence and has implications of sperm. Indeed, sperm retention is a part of Jing Gong training through sexual alchemy practice. However, it needs to be understood as more than sperm. It can also translate as flesh or tissue. Jing then means the body itself, and so cultivation of the body (Jing Gong) is an exercise to keep the body healthy, young, and strong. This exercise is done through innumerable ways such as health Qigong practices, stretching regimes, strength training, or, martial arts practice. It is old advice in so many martial arts and Qigong practices to avoid too much sex. Some traditions eschew sex entirely! This side of Jing Gong (translating here as essence or sperm) has roots within Traditional Chinese Medicine and the effect that production of sperm has on the Pre-heaven Qi (inherited or ancestral Qi) and on the body. Simply put, producing sperm takes a little bit of life force, so ejaculating more than recommended, can run a deficit and damage health and longevity. Some Taoist traditions went so far as to create schedules by age to tell cultivators how much they could ejaculate without causing damage to themselves.

Everything has a balance and we are looking for the achievement of stability. From a Taoist point of view, ejaculation is not harmful. It is a natural part of life and should not be removed from the lifestyle except for some extreme cases of training. The schedule they set out is that as we grow older, we should have sex less (which includes solo, if you know what I mean). In the twenties once per day is natural, thirties, once per three days, forties once per five days, fifties, once per week, and at sixty once per month. By the age of seventy, we are expected to be having no Sex. From researching and talking about this with friends who are Chinese Doctors, I have learned to be Taoist about the whole thing. Do you feel weak after sex? How long does it take to recover? Go with the flow and don't overtax yourself.

Rules of abstinence and generally come from traditions of Buddhist monasticism and so sex has a lot of attachment rolled up in it. Celibacy becomes more about removing attachments than health issues. Only in times of extreme training where the body is severely taxed is chastity prescribed by knowledgeable teachers who are not just repeating what their masters told them but are seeing what benefits students will get and how they will handle the training. My recommendation is to be natural, but I am admittedly Taoist in my way of thought.

However, there is one more note about all this in the modern world. The use of pornography counts as solo sex, and since the internet makes it so readily available, many people becoming addicted and over-sex themselves. Discussions of this are readily available so I will not go on and on about them here. Yin deficiency is a real problem and can severely shorten your lifespan and quality of life. Be aware of your own body and what effect sex has on you and you should be fine.

Moving up the diagram is Qi Xue, the Qi rooted in the Blood, the Qi of the body. Filling this basin through cultivation requires understanding of how to cultivate Qi. Qi is translated as energy, but a broader definition is relationship. Since all energy comes from a relationship between things, we can see how it encompasses the former definition. Regarding the three treasures diagram of Jing-Qi-Shen, Qi is the relationship between Jing and Shen, or in layman's terms the body or tissue or flesh and the mind or spirit. Qigong methods are all rooted in the study or relationships of one type or another and will help cultivate the strength of those relationships through training. On this model, Qigong is referring to the strengthening of the relationship between mind and body and so Qigong methods like Ba Duan Jin or Five Animal Frolics are perfect for this type of training. Of course, my own revolved around 18 Lohan Palm at this point so it was demonstrated to be an excellent method to cultivate Qi.

My teacher also taught me the standing and seated eight brocade Qigong alongside other methods as supplemental training.

Any general health Qigong will work correctly for this so long as you are observing the relationships in the body and between the mind and body. For example, in the Eight Brocade Qigong there are movements like Draw the Bow to Shoot the Eagle where these relationships are studied by feeling the opening of Tan Zhong (the chest) and Laogong (centre of the palm) while pulling the bowstring and pushing away the bow stave. The stance has weight requirements for the legs as well as where the weight should fall through the foot to the earth (Yong Quan). So, to do this movement well many relationships are looked at and worked to become more and more correct. This movement integrates the mind into the tissue and as such the relationship between mind and body strengthens, building Qi. Filling this basin will begin to overflow the flesh (Jing) as the body becomes stronger and healthier from the Qigong practice as well as upwards into the basin of the Shen as the mind becomes more focused and unambiguous about its intentions. The Martial arts cover this basin nicely. Besides learning Qigong methods, simply training for more power or accuracy or structure acquires excellent coordination of the mind and body.

The top basin of the lower diagram is Shen Xue, the spirit rooted in the blood. Here, Shen is made up of different parts and covers the Yi (Intellectual Mind), Yi (Intention of the Mind), Shen (Spirit or Soul) and Xin (Emotional Mind) among others. Shen is all the components of a human being that are ethereal, the reason we think and feel and have ideas. It is also the thoughts themselves, religious experiences, and the part that can look within and observe those thoughts. The Shen is being worked on while trying to answer questions like “Who is thinking?”

Looking deeply into the mind and heart is called Shen Gong (Training the Shen). Typically, these are the more esoteric practices or practices considered internal or Nei Gong. To differentiate between the two is not necessary but consider Shen Gong as training the soul and Nei Gong training the character.

Filling the basin of Shen is strengthening the mind and focusing it correctly. Itis easiest to do through methods of meditative practices or more advanced Qigong. Training the mind through meditation is through studying and quieting it so it can become focused and stronger over time. For instance, in Buddhist Qigong methods like the recitation of a mantra either silently or aloud, we study how long we can maintain a state of concentration before our minds wander. Over time and practice, this time lengthens, and our minds become more precise and stronger. Emotions become something we are not made to feel but something we see as natural and always allow a choice as to how we will use them. My meditation master Loung Phor referred to this as the emotional filter that we can see our emotions through as they arise but not be manipulated by them.

Esoteric Qigong refers to methods that are about studying relationships within the mind and relationships between reality and our perception of it. These are known as spiritual or alchemical Qigong, alchemical in the sense that they are a catalyst for the transformation of Shen. For example, simple forms of listening Qigong where you look outwards or inwards and really try to hear what is going on without your mind filtering the sound away is a type of this training. This removes the filter of the mind between reality and perception. A more advanced Qigong like Tien Shan studies your relationship to time and how you perceive it. Either of these offers a real chance for growth and as such strengthens Shen, filling the basin. When the basin of Shen is filled it trickles down to the Qi basin (relationships) and the Jing basin (the flesh and essence). Examples of this include people like aged monks who spend most of their time in meditation but remain healthy and youthful long into their advanced years.

Now the three treasures are defined and as is their interrelation in the lower half of the diagram. Each is a basin that needs to be filled through cultivation. Doing any one of the practices outlined will slowly fill all three of those basins, but the issue with this type of cultivation is time. Most people will reach the level of human maximum in this way just as the detrimental effects of old age start to work against them. My teacher said, "this is why it is normal human maximum. Almost no one goes above the line."

The easiest way to avoid the pitfall of age is to train and cultivate to fill all three basins at once. Therefore, the Chinese training methods often show a great deal of diversity. It is this reason martial arts are considered as a highly effective method for cultivation. A truly complete art has training material for all three basins and can be started young. Forms, drills, and exercises are for the Jing. Qigong methods cultivate strong Qi. And Meditative and Nei Gong practices cultivate Shen. It is why many of the highest regarded mythical figures in China like the Eight Immortals are associated with martial arts training and not just Qigong or meditation.

The Line of life was the next lesson in this topic and dealt with the line of health and longevity that can be mapped through the lower diagram of the three treasures. He drew a line from left to right across the lower diagram that represented birth to death and it looked something like this:

This diagram represents the life of a typical person who is cultivating and working to achieve what would be referred to as enlightenment throughout their lives. As they begin to get somewhere one of two things happens: 1) Either old age begins to degenerate the Jing (body) and begins its downward gradient into death or 2) They make a mistake in their cultivation which starts the downward slope from which they cannot recover. This does not necessarily kill them but at the very least it sets them back far enough they will never reach the maximum human line. These kinds of mistakes have been documented, and this is where Qigong sickness becomes an issue. At this point in my practice, he relayed to me a story about his older Gongfu brother who went to train under another Master in what he referred to as a Qigong cult.

So, my Sihing likes this other Master because he teaches fast, so he goes to learn his Qigong. A few months and I can see his Qigong is no good, but even though I am a doctor, he won't listen to me because I am his Si Dai (younger brother). I tell him not to train this way anymore. It's incorrect. Within six months he has fevers, another two months he went blind.

Shifu used this story as a warning to understand deeply what a Qigong or training method is about and to avoid a mistake that can not only cause illness but can remove any chance of moving up the diagram towards the higher levels of training. I have heeded his advice quite seriously since then and have made it essential to try and understand what I am doing before I undertake training. I recommend you do the same.

At the top half of the diagram the three treasures of Jing, Qi, and Shen are now preceded with Zheng (正), a character that translates as upright, honest, genuine, or authentic. In the Huang Di Nei Jing is the term Zheng Ren, True Human being, described as a state to aspire to through cultivation. The use of the character Zheng in this diagram differentiates the three treasures above the line from those below it. The Zheng (True) types of Jing, Qi, and Shen are those not rooted in the blood or the body but instead are about authentic and genuine cultivation. It is not the perspective from within us but examining reality around us and removing the filters and ideas that colour and prevent us from truly observing what is real and happening right now. It is without the dualism that we are separate from the whole, without the projection of our ideas and goals and paradigms onto reality itself.

The cultivation at this level becomes more external, related to the reality around us. It is the most challenging type of training to undergo because it must be brutal in its honesty and cutting in its insights. This level is esoteric training for most although it is just looking deeply into reality to observe and discover what we have done to cloud it from ourselves. True Jing (Zheng Jing) is the cultivation of the body and an understanding of its reality. It is knowing who you are and what your body is, realizing your genetic potential and limitations and knowing that judgment is not necessary. This level of cultivation is about removing the cultural ideals imposed upon us about how we look, what we weight and so on. But instead we are looking directly and cultivating directly towards our own best physicality. This is a significant part of longevity training as it begins to remove the production of stress hormones related to our physical insecurities and lets us be honest about how we should be cultivating and what makes up our bodies. Every bite of food we eat becomes what we are made of. Do you want to be made of processed sugars or nutrients? There are no judgments necessary. But, what do you plan to do? You are made of up the dust of stars and solar energy. Determine how clean it is to create your Jing.

Zheng Qi (True Qi) is a step upwards. The basin of True Jing must be filled to cultivate upwards into the Zheng Qi. Remember the definition of Qi is relationships. Zheng Qi is peeling away the mental constructs that keep us from seeing and interacting with reality directly. It is not just about our physicality, but it is the stage of training where Qigong exercises become strange, so it is misunderstood most of the time. These methods are not about gaining super abilities but about stripping away our preconceptions. Studying what we are in relationship to direct reality is an esoteric and challenging practice. Some examples of this kind of Qigong involve observations of time passing, the interconnection between living things, and so on.

Another line separated Zheng Qi from Zheng Shen when Shifu drew it for me on the chart. I asked him what it meant.

“Above this line, you will attract attention,” he said. “A student here will meet a teacher to help him move forward.” He then answered my other questions about what this meant, and the information became more understandable and at the same time more esoteric. Essentially, a teacher will appear in your life and help you move forward. Very few reach this level of cultivation, and fewer still can progress here without a teacher. He mentioned famous examples like Siddhartha Gautama Buddha as well as legendary figures like the Immortals Zhong Li Quan and Lu Dong Bin.

Zheng Shen is the True Shen or Spirit. From a strong cultivation of all the lower basins, the truth of reality is examined from a spiritual perspective, and it is the completion of this process that brings us to the top of the chart. I can say no more about it since I have not experienced this high-level understanding and only know that completion of this stage is what people call enlightenment, in the sense of a huge accomplishment, or Immortality. Study of the nature of reality from a perspective of oneness and interconnectedness removes the idea of self, and the paradox of “no-self and self” arises directly as Yin and Yang and will be held in the mind entirely and calmly seeing reality for what it is.

The top of the chart is Xu, Emptiness or the Void. The state of both being and not being. It is also Wu Ji the state of pure pregnant potential. The Yang of the chart, the ethereal, is the realm of the Buddhas and Immortals. Shifu mentioned at this point that in the stages of Immortality those who reach the top of this chart are considered the highest level of cultivation or Heavenly Immortals (Tien Shan) and leave this realm for Heaven.

# Iron Training Methods (鐵法)

by Sifu Neil Ripski

# Iron Training Methods (鐵法)

Iron-Body, Golden Bell Armour, Iron Vest, Iron Shirt, Cotton Belly, all different names of different methods, all aiming at the same results. Avoiding getting injured when struck in the torso. On the other side of the fence, we have the Iron-Palm, Iron Fist, Cotton Palm, Red Sand Palm and other methods, meant to cause massive damage from strikes. I find myself referring to these methods often when I am teaching or writing about other subjects and merely glossing over what they are and how to train them so now I am taking the time to look directly at them and what they are.

To discuss iron training correctly, we must establish there are two major schools of thought. You have Wai Gong and Nei Gong or External Methods and Internal Methods.

by Sifu Neil Ripski

# Wai Gong Methods (外功發)

Wai Gong training focuses on the exterior of the body through body hardening, muscularity, and toughness. These are the methods that, although they involve mental constructs during training, are essentially toughening up so you can take a punch. These types of Iron-Body training usually involve the Shaolin methods of being struck by bags of sand, groups of sticks or chopsticks, other training partners, or your own hands. Wai Gong methods mostly work the body from the outside in to gain the result desired. In my studies of the Chinese Martial Arts, I have come across different methods from the Wai Gong schools and will share some of them here.

## Iron Broom (Iron Legs) (鐵腿)

Iron Broom is a part of the Iron-Body training done explicitly to the shins to turn them into more formidable weapons. The result is also useful when using the shins to act as shields for the body. With all the following training routines, be sure to start off with the shins exposed, first rubbing up and down along the shins before starting, then slapping them up and down with the palms of the hands. Called Shao Lin Pai Fa 少林拍法 or Shaolin Patting method, it is used to prepare the body for training as well as cooling down the body after exercise.

## Shaolin Pai Fa (少林拍法)

Pai Fa has two purposes. First is to stimulate the Wei Qi which is essentially the body's exterior defensive mechanism, the protective Qi of the body that deals with external pathogens as well as blows. The patting or slapping stimulates the Wei Qi to become more active and by placing it under duress strengthens it just like exercising a muscle group. Wei Qi is also your immune system, so you can see the link between Iron-Body practices and increasing the health of the practitioner. Second, the patting method is done in a specific pattern meant to be confusing to the body, and so it does not become accustomed to blows dealt in a rhythm. With the practitioner's mind quiet, the pattern stimulates the body's Wei Qi to be at the ready like a soldier standing guard, ready for attack. The pattern is: 1-2-3 pause 1-2- 3 pause 1-2-3-4-5-6-7 pause, repeat. The Shaolin Pai Fa method is a complete Iron-Body method as well. If done as a beginner level exercise it should be all over the body from top to bottom back to top. Be sure to slap the body just hard enough to be slightly uncomfortable if doing it for this purpose. If you are using it only as a warm up or cool down after training the slapping should only be a slight sting from each palm. As a cool down method, the Pai Fa remains the same but with less power and with the purpose of sealing and storing the result of the training. In Internal Practices like Qigong or alchemy, the body opens to the outside world to transform training. The Pai Fa settles the body back into itself and is a good method to use to avoid external invasions, like cold, from seeping into the body.

## Iron Legs (Iron Broom) Tie Tui (鐵腿)

Initially, this training is using your own body to toughen the shins and then you advance to foreign objects. The first level is to sit with the shins exposed and begin with the Shaolin Pai Fa with enough force to be uncomfortable and the exposed skin turns red. Practice this way every day for a few minutes for at least fourteen days before moving on.

The second level of Iron Broom training uses a bundle of wooden chopsticks. Gather together a group of chopsticks just big enough to fit into your hand comfortably, and then add eight more. Lash them together with something, the bundle we use at my school is bound with thick rubber bands which works well. Sit with the legs exposed and begin with a few Pai Fa to warm up the legs and get the Wei Qi awake then switch to the bundle of chopsticks. Tap up and down the shins for a few minutes until it is too uncomfortable to continue. Now, remember that you are not striking the bone in the shin directly but instead striking so the brunt of the force lands on the outside of the shin bone on Tibialis Anterior with only some of the surface of the chopsticks hitting the shin bone. It is Tibialis Anterior that must be developed to deal and take damage as much as, if not more so than the shin bone itself. Train in this way for at least thirty days.

The third level of the iron broom training uses a round object like a bottle or a rolling pin. This part of the exercise is painful, and most people do not progress steadily enough to handle it. There is no reason to rush this training, especially in the case of body hardening exercises. To rush the development is to put yourself at risk of long-term damage. So, if you like being able to walk comfortably and pain-free, do not skip levels. If this level is too awful to train, go back to the chopsticks for another few weeks before trying again. Train slowly and carefully, and results will appear without detrimental effects. After warming up the legs with Pai Fa and then a hundred strikes with the chopsticks, roll the pin up and down the shin bone. This part of the training is for the bone itself and as such should be done with caution, gently at first and then applying more pressure as you train. Roll the legs for a few minutes and then cool down again using the Pai Fa to bring blood to the area to help heal, seal and store. Train this way as your upkeep from this point on but after at least thirty days you can start kicking things your shins gently to see your accomplishment in the skill. If you have partners to train with and they too are working on this skill you can prepare by clashing shins together over and over during a training session. This one is popular in my school among the students who are working on this skill as it allows them a sense of competition and accomplishment. Be careful.

I have had a couple of students take this training to a high level, and they find that kicking their shins through wooden staffs or baseball bats becomes quite easy. One of my first students took a real liking to iron skills and demonstrated kicking through a two-inch diameter staff on more than one occasion.

# Iron Arms Training (鐵臂法)

## San Xing (三星)

The methods described for Iron Broom can be done on the arms in the same way. However, there are a couple of extra techniques in this training. The most common is Three Stars Arm Banging, San Xing (三星) done with a partner.

Standing facing one another the two players begin by striking the top of the forearms together, right hand on the right-hand side by turning the torso. The striking surface here is the outside or Yang side of the forearm and strikes both the radius and the ulna. The second star or strike is done upwards with the palms facing up and the forearms clashing on the radius (thumb) side. The third strike is done downwards with the palm facing the ground and the forearms striking on the ulna (little finger) side of the forearm. This training should be done slowly and carefully before building up to more power and speed. Cool down with the Shaolin Pai Fa and then use Dit Da Jow to avoid injuries that could stop tomorrow's training.

## Praying Mantis Forearm Grinding (螳螂磨骨)

Another method I learned from a Shifu of Northern Praying Mantis is called Forearm Grinding. Warm up and bring blood to the forearms by closing the fist and bending the wrist forward while flexing the forearm with great force. The training requires an apparatus such as a table countertop or bench, something that is sturdy and has a solid top When I learned this, I was at his grocery store in Chinatown and he taught it to me on the herbal dispensary counter. With all the force you can manage, place the palm side of the forearm near the elbow on the edge of the desk and drag it back while pressing down into the edge of the table. When the wrist is reached, turn the arm over, palm out, and push it back away from you from wrist to elbow. Press all the while, so the edge of the counter drags on the forearm the entire way. Repeat until you can stand no more and then cool down with Pai Fa and use Dit Da Jow. It is a bit extreme, but this method results in muscular and hard forearms. I saw this Shifu demonstrate receiving strikes from a shovel handle just using the underside of his forearms, and I was not swinging lightly!

## Praying Mantis Forearm Striking Method (螳螂骨擊法)

The Ma Family style also has a small praying mantis system, and it has its apparatus training for iron forearms. Take two sawhorses or benches to act as support legs for the apparatus at waist height, attach a flexible stick or staff across the top. Stand in Horse Stance or Tang Lang Bu (螳螂步) (Praying Mantis Stance) and strike the staff with the bottom, side, and top of the forearm, one at a time. The flexibility of the stick is critical here as a stick too hard will cause damage or injury to the arms if struck too hard. A piece of green, fresh, bamboo is traditional but since that is not always available, a flexible staff like a new cut sapling from the forest or staff made of wax wood or rattan will work just as well. After training rub the arms with as much pressure as you can. Use the Pai Fa method and Dit Da Jow to help heal for the next day's training.

## Iron Bar Rolling (鐵桿滾)

A common Wai Gong exercise for conditioning the forearms uses an Iron bar or sometimes a small log. Roll the bar down the forearms with the arms stretched out in front of you then tossing it into the air and catching it again and again on the forearms to work and condition them to strikes. To quote Logan, a friend of mine, "Train don't strain." Be careful with this exercise and be sure to heal each day to avoid damage to the bones of the arm. A more modern variant I have seen of this uses a metal pipe with some sand inside and the ends capped, this makes the weight adjustable and mobile during the exercises.

## Ma Family Methods (馬家法)

I am labelling the methods my teacher taught me as Ma Family methods. Not only is that their unique lineage but they tend to have a unique flavour and different training than most Shaolin methods I have come across. I am doing this not only to give credit to where I received my training but to help keep the Ma Family style alive amongst people who end up training their methods. They are neither better nor worse than any of the other techniques in this writing, just different.

## Ma Family Tiger Bone Method (馬家虎骨法)

The Ma family tiger system uses an apparatus in Wai Gong iron forearm training as well. Like most old methods of practice, it is simple to find or make. Use a log about three to four feet long and about four to six inches in diameter. Place it on your forearms with your arms outstretched, palms facing one another. Start with the log cradled at the elbow and roll it down towards your wrists. Reach the wrist toss it into the air and catch it with the forearms and roll it back to the elbows. Repeat until you can stand no more. Cool down with the Pai Fa and use Dit Da Jow to be able to heal for the next day's training.

Depending on where you live you may find it difficult to acquire a log, my Shifu used a steel pipe for the training at home as it was easy to purchase from any hardware store. I have also seen other lineages with a similar apparatus using a pipe with sand or some steel shot inside it with the ends capped for this training, which will make it even less pleasant.

## Ma Family Iron Fist (馬家鐵拳)

Iron Fist training is disguised as part of the beginning student's workout at first. It contains three levels of conditioning. The first level is, after warming up, Tiger push-ups on the fists. From a push-up position press yourself back onto your feet and raise your buttocks in the air. Lower your head towards your fists and without touching the earth bring yourself through your hands with your shoulders and push up into a cobra-like position. Repeat as many times as possible each day until it becomes simple. We practice this until 45 could be done quickly before moving to the next stage. After finishing, cool down with the Shaolin patting method and utilize Dit Da Jow to help the hands to heal.

The second level is punching a stack of paper attached or hung from a wall. Be sure the wall is sturdy enough for you to strike it without damaging it. We would use a phone book with the covers torn off. Strike the paper stack with a good deal of force many times each day. Any pages torn off from your punching are left off the pile until eventually you are striking the bare wall. Massage the hands and fingers and cool down with the Shaolin patting method before putting on Dit Da Jow to heal up. Repeat this training daily until there is no phone book left.

The final stage of the training starts with leaning against the wall on your fist. Gradually work up to handstands on your fists, and the highest part of this is a single arm handstand on the fist. At this level, we could start punching hard objects like trees or stones. I got a piece of granite tombstone from a local business and stood it up to strike. The most important thing in this hard of training is a methodical approach. Do not injure your hands or break your knuckles. Work up slowly and gently and even when punching the stone be sure to progress gradually. I was able to work up to 1000 strikes a day on the rock which I carried on for a few years. The results were fantastic and even now that I choose to train other things my fists remain quite hard.

When training this method of iron fist, any time you exercise power through your fists by striking or even tiger pushups be sure to exhale and lead the Qi from Dantian through Tan Zhong (Chest centre) also known as middle Dantian (中田丹 Zhong Dantian) to the Laogong (劳宫) points in the fists themselves. Bring attention to this area of the body consciously through Yi Ling Qi (the mind leads the Qi) as well as unconsciously through the actions of the training. Exhale when hitting or delivering force and inhale to Dantian in between those moments.

## Ma Family Iron-Palm (馬家鐵沙掌)

The Ma family Iron-Palm is almost the same progression as the Iron Fist training above. Begin with tiger push-ups on the palms, progress to striking either a phone book or a bag filled with sand attached to the wall. These are the first two levels and should be progressed through carefully and slowly before moving on.
The differences in the training start here at level three, standing a short distance from a wall, lean into the wall with just your fingertips holding you. As you exhale, drop your palms onto the wall. Drive force from your shoulders into it. Go back onto your fingertips and repeat until tired. After a couple of weeks at this level, you should find that you can strike with great force with little movement.

Here the training switches to a more internal approach. Standing or sitting in front a hanging bag filled with sand or small stones and from this position calm your mind. Lead the Qi from Dantian to the palms of the hands, as though the hands were in hot water and getting warmer and warmer. Keep the fingers up and the palms facing away from you while you exhale into the palms of the hands, do not lead the Qi from the palms of the hands just into them, filling them and making them hotter and hotter. When you feel a sensation of heat or tingling, strike the bag with both of your palms. Repeat this cycle each day at least 36 times. This practice is also done standing over an Iron-Palm bag or stone and repeat with the hand dropping on to the rock for the strike, one hand at a time.

Cool down with the Shaolin patting method and Guan Qi Fa.

## Ma Family Iron Nail (馬家鐵釘)

Iron Nail is training the fingers to strike. The process is again the same as the iron fist method, starting with tiger push-ups on the fingertips. When this becomes easy, begin training regular push-ups on the fingertips and start trying to invert yourself. When push-ups on the fingertips become easy, get a bucket and fill it with sand. Strike the fingertips into the sand over and over each day until you can bury your fingers entirely in the sand without pain. From here work on handstands on your fingertips and at advanced levels begin using fewer fingers until you are only the tips of the index fingers or even a single digit. My Shifu had this skill, and he told me it took him ten years to accomplish the single arm single finger handstand. On one occasion, I witnessed his ability to drive his finger into someone's body.

Be sure to massage the fingers with Dit Da Jow and spend time keeping them warm and able to heal.

## Ma Family Dog Skin Palm (狗的皮掌)

Literally, Dog Leather Palm, it is one of those skills that seems like it is from an old Shaw Brothers movie from the 1970's. The training method is quite simple and has a great ability associated with it, but the name comes from the traditional apparatus used for training. In the past when dogs were raised for meat in China an Iron-Palm style bag would be made from the dog hide, stuffed with beans and with the dog's hair still intact (on the leather). The bag should be much larger than your hand and quite substantial in modern times, if you don't live somewhere that dog is eaten, an Iron-Palm bag filled with heavy stones, steel BBs, or sand will work fine.

Place the bag on a table top and nearer to the centre of the table than then edge. Be sure the table is sturdy enough to take a firm strike from your palm without breaking and then strike the bag with an open palm slap. Without grabbing it with your fingers, drag the bag to the edge of the table. Ideally, do this in one smooth motion, and you will be able to drag a considerable weight towards you. You should also train this on your forearms, hitting the bag with the bottom of your forearm and pulling it towards you with only that point of contact. Heavier is better in this case and the bag may need to be able to be increased in weight. When you can drag in one motion 50 lbs or more you will have a right amount of this skill.

In combative application dog skin palm in meant to do one of two things. One, it gives you the ability to drag an opponent off balance without using your hands to attach to them. And two, it gives you the ability to tear flesh from them with a slap. The traditional bag made of dog skin was used to rip the hair off the bag with the palm by dragging. An accomplished master would be able to slap an opponent's face and drag or tear the flesh from their cheeks.

## Ma Family Rubbing Ink Palm / Black Ink Palm (墨黑掌)

Calligraphy ink was traditionally stored in small sticks that needed to be rubbed on a wet stone to make the ink usable. The act of rubbing the ink, Ca Mo (擦墨), required pressure and circular movements on the ink stone to make the ink. This reference is widespread in Chinese martial arts as it was once a part of everyday life that people could readily understand. In the case of the Rubbing Ink Palm or Black Ink Palm, it refers to the pressure needed to drag the ink from the ink stone and so is much like the dog skin palm described above.

Black Ink Palm comes from the small system of Snake boxing taught by the Ma family and refers to the ability to grab and drag an opponent with the forearms, keeping the hands free. Training black ink palm is simple. Traditionally a tree or post would be used although in modern times we use the type of self-standing heavy bag filled with water in the base.

Stand in front of the post and rub it with the insides of your forearms, trying to drag the post towards you. Rub it with as much force as you can without tearing your flesh and work on the adhering power in the Yin flesh of the arms. Move around freely and rub the post in all directions using different stepping methods. The traditional way used in this drill from the family had a stepping pattern known as Diamond Stepping which was merely to rotate around the post changing from a cross step stance, Niu Bu (扭步), to an open, small horse stance, Ma Bu (馬步), and repeating the step to circle the post, being sure to train both directions. Use Dit Da Jow to help recover from bruising but using it on open wounds is not recommended. Rub the arms after training to help remove blood stagnation in the arms.

## **Yin Flesh Dragging Method (陰肉磨法)**

This method is the least favourite among my students and with good reason. It is the most painful of all the iron arm exercises except maybe the Praying Mantis bone grinding method. Stand across from a partner in horse stance. Both of you turn the waist and bring the right hands toward one another slapping with your palm just below the elbow on the inside of the forearm. The more surface area of the palm that hits the inside of the partner's forearm, the better. Once the strike has hit the forearm of the partner, drag it with high pressure down the Yin flesh of the inside of the forearm towards their wrist while they do the same. Repeat on both sides. Be sure to use the Pai Fa method to gently cool down the area and use Dit Da Jow to heal up.

This method teaches or conditions the inside of the forearm for Iron-Body resiliency but the dragging and pulling of the flesh should be done without the use of the fingers. Through pressure, you can attach and drag your palm down their flesh in a sticky, connected way. This method is a type of specialized Iron-Palm used to connect to the opponent's flesh and scrape it in such a way as to tear it during the strike. Another method that also trains this skill is Dog Skin Palm.

# Iron-Body Methods (鐵體法)

The Iron-Body here is referring to the conditioning of the torso to protect and cover the organs which are a significant target in traditional Chinese Martial Arts. The ideal in pre-fire-arm martial arts was to be able to kill an opponent as quickly and effectively as possible. From a modern biomedical point of view, this means that the strikes had to be able to deal lethal damage to the opponent's internal organs. With many people training striking methods like Iron-Palm, designed to do just that, Iron-Body methods as a sort of armour became a must. The torso required conditioning to handle the abuse other people were learning to dish out.

## Shaolin Body Beating (少林體擊法)

There are many different Wai Gong Iron-Body training methods, but first I will discuss the body beating method from Shaolin tradition. Much like the iron broom methods discussed before these are meant to arouse the Wei Qi and harden the muscularity of the body through constant abuse. The first level of body beating is again the Shaolin Pai Fa patting method on yourself. Expose the torso and slap using the Pai Fa at a borderline uncomfortable level. Ideally, a training partner will be around to slap the back of the body for you and you for them. Move from this level after a few weeks of being hit to bean filled bags instead of the hands. These are usually constructed as one to two-foot-long cylindrical bags filled with mung beans and are used the same way striking the body while flexing the muscularity on impact used in the same way as hands. Be sure to try and hit your entire torso with the bag. After two more weeks, you can move up to harder substances in the bag like sand or small gravel.

Traditionally you will find directions to use things like iron or lead shot. I would stay away from these just because lead poisoning is a real possibility and materials that are dense can easily fracture the ribs. Other Nei Gong methods can bring you past the level of sandbags. Training this method for 100 days will allow you to understand what the benefit is and see it manifest in your body. There are many different Iron-Body methods in the Wai Gong schools that involve similar routines of training. Be sure to use the Shaolin Pai Fa to warm up and cool down after exercise and Dit Da Jow if needed to heal for the next day's practice.

## Xinyi Liuhe Iron-Body (心意六合拳身體擊球)

Xinyiliuhe is still a rare art in most of the world since it was only released into the broader public by Yu Hualong in the 1980's after a long adventurous life. The ten styles or ten animals Xinyi is famous for its violent, aggressive methods and its different training principles, eschewing forms for repetitive drills and two-person work. Its method of Iron-Body training known in English as Xinyi Body Banging is a partner exercise that conditions the bodies of both partners simultaneously through striking It is made up of five different striking areas, the upper arm, chest, shoulder back, ribs and buttocks.

Partners stand facing one another and at the moment of impact, regardless of the body area exhale sharply to remove air from the lungs and avoid damage from the compression of the chest during impact. Many people about to be struck hold their breath, which is one thing this is meant to train out of the practitioner. In the worst-case scenarios, lungs can burst under pressure from a massive attack when holding the breath.

### The Bear Arm (Upper Arm) (熊臂)

Holding the wrist of the opposite arm, partners step into one another striking the upper arm of each person. The striking area should be the flat between the bicep and triceps on the outside of the arm, banging into one another with force while exhaling. The partners then step back from one another and step in on the other side working both sides equally.

## Chest (胸部)

Moving the arms out of the way the partners step into one another and strike on the pectoral (side of the chest) on each other while exhaling. Be sure to flex and push the chest forward as you hit the other person and exhale sharply. This technique teaches the ability to bounce power off the body by moving into instead of away from it. Bounce each other's force from each strike, repeat equally on both sides.

## Shoulder (Back) (肩)

This strike is on the back of the shoulder, including the shoulder blade which should be sunken and flat with the rest of the back. The partners step past one another, for example, the right foot steps forward on both people, and lean back with their right shoulders turning into one another and striking with the rear of the shoulder while exhaling. The partners then step back from one another and repeat on the other side. Be sure to keep the shoulders down and settled properly, or you will be hitting the bone of the shoulder blade only. The whole muscularity and structure of the upper back are meant to be conditioned.

## Ribs (肋骨)

People tend to have a difficult time with this one. The striking area is the side of the rib cage and latissimus dorsi at the same time. Lifting the arms above the head the partners step into one another and lean forward and sideways to open the rib cage to strike. The feet here must step to the inside of to wind the bodies together for the impact. Be sure to bounce the force off your body and exhale sharply. The impact goes directly into the lungs and can cause a good deal of damage if done incorrectly. Step back from each strike and change sides, training both sides equally.

## Buttocks (臀部)

Stepping past the partner slightly sideways striking each other with the buttocks using a hip motion to bounce the force off one and into one another. The hands stay in front of the body or over the head to be out of the way. Flex the buttocks as they are struck, this is important as I find many students do not have much conscious control of the buttocks in this exercise and end up hurting their pelvis. It is conditioning the muscularity of the buttocks, not the bones. Exhale sharply and train both sides equally stepping backwards from the partner and repeating on the other side.

Traditionally there is a stepping pattern with the motion called Swallow Skims the Water but for the conditioning itself, it is not necessary. Train and progress slowly to avoid injury and be sure to exhale on every strike to the body.

## Baguazhang Iron-Body (八卦章鐵體)

Baguazhang training has many benefits. Practitioners and Masters write and speak about the Iron-Body it creates merely from the correct practice of Circle Walking. In my experience, I have seen the benefits of this training for Iron-Body, but in the form of the written word, it would be too complex. That type of Iron-Body would also be considered Nei Gong as it works from the inside of the body to the outside through the various kinds of torque and twisting. Instead, I will discuss the Wai Gong methods of Bagua Iron-Body that train from the exterior to the interior through easily understood drills.

## Solo Method (獨法)

This Iron-Body method comes from the Cheng Style of Baguazhang handed down from Cheng Ting Hua through Shifu Yang Guo Tai. I would also recommend this training for the Wei Qi (Protective Qi) essentially the immune system. Through training this method, the immune system increases in strength, it is this method I teach and use in the fall and winter in my Taiji and Qigong classes with some students over 80 years old!

As with other methods, there needs to be a sharp exhalation of the breath on each blow. In this case it should be through the nose. Be sure to blow your nose ahead of time and perhaps have a handkerchief on you as you train. You do tend to end up wearing your snot. Gross, but it works.

Standing with the feet shoulder width apart, ball up the fists with the thumb atop the forefinger as though you were knocking on a door. It is the knocking surface of the hand that you will be striking with, not just your knuckles but the whole flat surface of the hand and fingers. As with other methods, this is a bouncing type of Iron-Body, and the torso should move into the strikes as they hit. Move the chest, abdomen, and kidneys into the direction of the attacks to bounce the power off the torso and train the body to move into force instead of away from it.

The striking pattern is to first hit the chest on the right pectoral, then the left side of the chest once each. Strike your right breast with your left fist and your left chest with your right fist, exhaling sharply through the nose each time. Then with both fists strike the upper abdomen bouncing the power off by moving into the strike, next hit the middle of the abdomen and then the lower abdomen below the navel in the same way. Now change your hand position to knife edge hand and strike with both hands into the inguinal crease joint while moving the hips forward into the power. The final strike in the pattern is on the kidneys Strike with the back of the hands in fists while moving the torso back into the power from the strike. To avoid bruising, do not hit the kidneys overly hard.

Each repetition of the pattern then is seven strikes- chest, chest, upper abs, middle abs, lower abs, Kua, kidneys. Repeat as many times as you feel comfortable with and with only the level of force you can handle easily, remember training is about training every day. If you need more than a day to recover, you were hitting too hard. Finish the method after the repetitions with the Shaolin Pai Fa as a cool down. If you require Dit Da Jow for this method, you have been striking too hard on the body to heal each night.

## Apparatus Method (設備法)

Here the apparatus refers to anything you can run in to with force. Trees, walls and posts work best. Be sure that the equipment is sturdy enough you're not going to cause any damage to it, or the attached structure. Throwing your body against the walls of your apartment is an excellent way to get evicted. Exhale forcefully and sharply through the nose when striking the post or wall and bounce the force from your body on each strike. Move the area of the body forcefully into the wall or post, not just running into it.

## Strike the Back (打回)

Stand with the heels a short distance away from the wall with your back facing the wall you are going to strike. Sit down into a Horse Stance, Ma Bu (馬步), stretch your arms forwards, you round out the back, and lean into the wall, all simultaneously. Sharply exhale as you hit the wall and if you do it right the impact coupled with the forward stretching of the arms should stand you back up to where you started. Repeat until you have had enough and be sure to keep the neck stretched upwards to avoid injuries to it.

## Carp Jumps from the Water (跳魚水)

Stand sideways to the wall with the side of the foot touching it while the other foot is off the wall and behind in a short Bow Stance, Gong Bu (弓步). Crouch down with your arm nearest the wall in a massive chop position and suddenly stand up and lift your arm out of the way of the ribs. Strike the rib cage into the wall each time. Sharply exhale as you hit and bounce your ribcage into the wall on the standing portion of the exercise. Crouch down and train your heavy chopping fist (重斬拳) on each repetition. Train equally both sides of the body.

## Ox Hits the Post (Tree) (牛撞樹)

Stand in front of a post or tree and step into the post with the pectorals, first one side then the other. It is the same point on the chest used in Xinyi Liuhe body banging. Strike the post with your pectoral and sharply exhale while bouncing the power off your body. Repeat equally on both sides.

## Partner Work (工作夥伴)

Baguazhang also has body hardening methods for partners. These are similar to the San Xing (Three Stars) arm banging training mentioned above, while circle-walking with a partner. There are many variants of this including turning and spinning into your partner to strike, but they all have the same theme. Between all these Bagua methods you already have tools to condition the back, chest, abs, ribs and now the arms with San Xing. Add to this the benefits of Circle walking training as mentioned earlier, and you have an excellent system of Iron-Body.

## Dit Da Jow (跌打酒) Fall Hit Wine

There is a great deal of discussion and entire businesses based on the making and selling of the seemingly magical Chinese Potion known as Dit Da Jow (Cantonese) or Die Da Jiu (Mandarin). There are dozens of recipes passed down through different families and styles. They are kept hidden from the main body of students and the public for various reasons but whatever the case the herbal liniments that fall in this category always come up whenever someone discusses the iron training of any kind.

First, the question of need for Dit Da Jow arises. Is it necessary to have it to train at all? You must understand what the purpose of the formulas is, which is healing the damage done to the body by training. Different bodies, different training methods, even different climates mean different uses of herbs. If you are training in a technique that causes enough damage that you cannot train the next day because you are not healed enough, then you need a supplement to help you and for this Jow is most often the answer. There is nothing secret about the potions. They are a result of solid Chinese Medical Herbology based on diagnosis and in many cases hundreds of years of trial and error over perhaps thousands of students. These secret formulas have been found to work and so if it isn't broke, don't fix it.

However, a competent TCM practitioner who knows their herbs would be able to create a custom formula for you as well. You don't necessarily need Grand Master so and so's secret formula to do the training. It's medicine. Understand what you are putting on or in some cases, in your body and keep training. My recommendation is to contact plumdragonherbs.com and get a good formula that you can make yourself and have ready for your training. Apply the Jow each day after practice and if you are still not healing fast enough, train a little less hard. Apply the Jow in the morning and after training and worry more about the exercise instead of the magical thinking about Dit Da Jow.

Making Jow is a simple matter. Once you have the herbal ingredients for your formula to make one gallon of Dit Da Jow, find a glass jar for ageing the wine. Put in the herbal formula and then the gallon of alcohol. It should be 40-60% abv, traditionally rice wine but I tend to use vodka or tequila which carries the herbs through the skin a touch smoother. Store it in the dark and shake it whenever you think of it. To age it faster, warm the alcohol to a temperature where it is just too hot to touch but not boiling and pour it into the jar with the herbs. Store it for at least three months before using it for training. I try to do a one-year minimum.

Here is a formula I use often, purchased from Plum Dragon, and made at home:

**Ku Yu Cheong Iron-Palm Jow** (Full Formula)

Zi Ran Tong (Pyrite) 18 grams
Hong Hua (Safflower) 18 g
Long Gu (Dragon Bone) 18 g
Wei Ling Xian (Clematis) 15 g
Wu Jia Pi (Acanthopanax Bark) 15 g
Bai Hua She (Pit Viper) 15 g
Ru Xiang (Frankincense) 15 g
Tu Bie Chong (Wingless Cockroach) 15 g
Su Mu (Sappan Wood) 15 g
Wu Ling Zhi (Squirrel Droppings) 12 g
Dang Gui Wei (Angelica Root Tail) 12 g
Xu Duan (Dipsacus Root) 12 g
Bai Zhi (White Angelica) 12 g
Xue Jie (Dragon Blood) 12 g
Gui Zhi (Cinnamon Twig) 12 g
Bai Shao (White Peony) 12 g
San Qi (Pseudoginseng) 12 g

Mu Xiang (Aucklandia Root) 12 g
Qiang Huo (Notopterygium) 12 g
Fang Feng (Siler Root) 12 g
Chi Shao (Red Peony) 12 g
Kuan Jin Teng (Tinospora Stem) 12 g
Ze Lan (Bugleweed) 12 g
Tao Ren (Peach Kernel) 12 g
Mu Tong (Akebia) 9 g
Rou Gui (Cinnamon Bark) 9 g
Gua Lou Ren (Trichosanthes Seed) 9 g
Shou Gong San (Harvest the Training Powder)

Another great formula I have used for Iron-Body training, specifically, Yi Jin Jing 易筋經 (Muscle Tendon Changing Classic) is Shou Gong San (Harvest the Training Powder/Wine) which is an internal and external formula and cheaper to make.

**Shou Gong San** (Harvest the Training Powder/Wine)

Dang Gui (Angelica) 1.5 ounces
Chen Pi (Aged Citrus Peel) 1 oz
Chen Xiang (Aquilaria Wood) 1 oz
Hong Hua (Safflower)- 1 oz
Jiang Xiang (Rose Wood) 0.5 oz
Zhi Shi (Immature Citrus Fruit) 0.5 oz
Tao Ren (Peach Kernel) 0.5 oz

# Nei Gong Methods (內功)

Nei Gong is a term used in many different contexts today. Literally, the first character Nei (內) means inside or within. The second character Gong (功) is made up of two radicals, on the left we have 工 (also pronounced gong) representing a carpenter's square, a measuring tool for exact work. The character on the right, 力 (pronounced Li), means force, strength, or work. So, Gong (功) translates as skilled labour or work. Measured Strength, or the intelligent use of effort. The terminology Nei Gong means the specialized skills and training used with an effort to acquire something within or from within.

I tend to use this terminology to refer to practices that refine the inner self or the character of the person such as learning not to lie to ourselves and discover who we truly are, so we can become True Human Beings. However, in this context Nei Gong practices for Iron-Body and Palm are methods that work from the inside to the exterior. So, rather than outside stimuli like striking the body with sticks or running into walls, the practice uses dynamic tensions, Qigong training, or Innervation.

## About Internal Training (內法)

Internal training involves some Qigong practices that can be dangerous, so I want to discuss Qigong training. Qi (氣) is usually defined as life energy or something akin to it and while energy is a possible way of looking at Qi it is a small translation of the concept. Qi is better understood to mean relationship. All types of Qi are types of relationships and energy is released or used through relationships, so we can see energy works but can be limiting. Instead, Qigong translates to the study of relationships, of which there are myriad: the joints of the body, posture to alignments, the temperature of the body, your relationships between your mind and body, or between you and the outside world. Some Qigong are meant to help you understand your relationships with reality and some are about the physicality. Most are a mixture of the two. Some of the Ma Family Qigong involve changing your relationship to your flesh in ways that transform the body. Often these Qigong involve visualizations, which is where the danger lies.

## Fire Chasing Demons (Qigong Sickness) (追火妖) (氣功病)

People who suffer from Qigong sickness are known as Fire Chasing Demons and most often suffer from improper instruction and guidance from a teacher. Fire Chasing refers to chasing after sensations that come from training Qigong. Sensations during Qigong can and do happen and are considered Yang events and are not directly dangerous or unhealthy. It is when the practitioner tries to recreate feelings, they have had in the past over and over again, so they can feel the energy by doing so, they become focused on feeling and experiencing things they create rather than doing their training! Qigong practice is not about the feeling of Qi. It is about the transformation and education that comes from the training itself, not the sensations that arise from it. So, you can see how easily a person can misstep into chasing fire through Qigong practice. Visualization practices are the most difficult as they ask the practitioner to use their minds to create sights, visions, and feelings for their transformative effects. Let go of the feeling each time you train, and if you do not have the same sense each time do not try to recreate the effect. Observe what takes place and live each moment of it without expectations of any particular feelings. In this way Qigong sickness should not be a problem. If you get any signs of it, see a Chinese Doctor and tell them about your Qigong practice.

When I trained with my teacher, I became an inner door student early on and moved into his home when I had financial trouble. During the years I lived with him I was made a disciple and learned the secret training methods including the fire-breathing Qigong, which is used a great deal in the Ma family Qigong practices. My personality is compulsive when it comes to training martial arts, so when I learned the Fire Qigong, I started training it daily, most of the time unsupervised. The Qigong creates a great deal of heat in the body that starts at Dantian (丹田) and moves and expands throughout the body. The skin sweats, and the palms turn red. As a young man, this feeling of power and a visceral confirmation of Qi was addictive to me, and it drove me to train more and more. The issue started I did not understand that remaining unattached to the sensations from the Qigong would allow the body to normalize and that the sensations would change over time. Instead, as the sensations became more familiar to me and seemed less powerful, I used more and more mind intent to make the feeling of the fire more intense each time. It was my mistake. Within a few months of this, I began to see fire symptoms in my body. In the afternoons I had headaches and a red face, which continued to grow until I had a headache every day and migraines once or twice a week. It was disabling. I tried different headache remedies and made visits to the western doctor. It continued, and I did not make the connection to the training for far too long. At night, I had incredible heat in my hands, feet, and heart sometimes known as Five Hearts Fire, a severe Qigong sickness. Living in this way was terrible, and my life was severely affected. When I learned of the cause, I stopped training the fire Qigong and worked almost exclusively on another Qigong from my teacher called Water Breathing Qigong. That, coupled with meditative practices, corrected the issue over a year or more. It is because of this experience that I take teaching Qigong very seriously and Qigong sickness is no longer just a theoretical possibility to me. No matter what Qigong you train, observe the sensations. Do not chase or create them. I was lucky, and I no longer have the headaches or heat at night. But Qigong sickness can result in severe and life-threatening conditions like Bone Steaming Fever in which the practitioner's bones feel as though they are on fire. It is incredibly painful. To western biomedicine, it appears as leukemia. Be safe and train smartly.

## Qi Regulation Method (Guan Qi Fa) (貫氣法)

This is a simple Qigong that has a profound effect on the body. It smooths and regulates the Qi and it can be used as a standalone Qigong or as a cool down after completing other Qigong methods, especially ones that are intense like some Iron-Body Qigong. It is not dangerous and is applicable daily, year-round.

Stand with the feet parallel and shoulder width apart. Bring the arms out from the sides and above the head as you inhale. Exhale with the palms pressing down along the front centerline of the body. On the first breath bring your mind from the Bai Hui (百會) point on the top of the head down the front of the body to Dantian (田丹). On the second breath out bring your mind down the back of the body from Bai Hui, down the back of the neck, down the spine, and to the tailbone. The third and final breath bring your mind through the centre of the body from Bai Hui down between the halves of the brain and down in front of the spine (Chong Mai) to Hui Yin (會陰). From here bisect the mind into the legs down the centre of the legs to the soles of the feet at Yongquan (湧泉).

## Ma Family Fire Breathing (馬家火氣功)

This Qigong was considered secret and is dangerous. Regarding visualization Qigong and fire chasing, this practice is responsible for my worst Qigong experience. The Qigong is powerful and works quite well but must come with a caveat, be aware that sensations change as the body naturalizes to them and become less intense. The fire or heat you feel when you first practice this Qigong will lessen over time. As a responsible Qigong practitioner or teacher, you should observe what you are feeling or not feeling and do the training without trying to increase or cause the feeling to begin or become more intense. Otherwise, it will lead to Qigong sickness.

Sit in a cross-legged or lotus position or standing in Ma Bu (馬步) (Horse Stance) with the body aligned vertically. Begin Buddhist style breathing and settle and clear the mind for a short time. If seated, place the palms of the hands (Lao Gong) on the knees connecting the heart and kidney meridians. If standing, place the hands over Dantian making a diamond with the thumbs and fingers around Qi Hai.

With the eyes slightly open and downcast, tongue touching the roof of the mouth, open the lips slightly and begin longer audible exhalations than inhalations. Pausing slightly at the end of each exhalation. Concentrate the mind on Dantian and see it like a hot coal in a fire. On each exhalation the audible breath is visualized to be blowing on the burning coal and making it grow in heat while the contraction of the belly condenses the heat into a single point. With each breath, the coal grows hotter and hotter, and that heat expands throughout the body. Do not practice this longer than 36 breaths. After training, sit or stand as you began and let the breathing and the mind settle back into a state of relaxation. No longer visualize anything and experience the body sorting out what the practice has done. Maintain this at least twice if you practiced. If the method was standing, walk around slowly and maintain a calm mind before continuing with your day.

Pair this practice with the Ma Family Water Breathing Qigong equally, which can be done directly afterwards instead of walking or sitting, to avoid creating an imbalance in the body.

## Breathing Fire & Water (Double Pause Breathing) (消防及水的呼吸)

It is essential to understand the roles of Fire and Water in the body and how to affect them through these Qigong. Fire-breathing Qigong is considered Yang, active, hot, etc. and Water Breathing Qigong the opposite (Yin). Both methods use visualizations and hand movements but there is a deeper level to understand cultivation of the elemental energies in the body through the cycle of the breath.

Consider the breathing cycle as having two distinct parts, inhalation and exhalation, Yin (陰) and Yang (陽) when compared to one another. Now, when an inhalation ceases and becomes exhalation, breathing pauses. I use the word pause here rather than stop because we are not consciously holding the breath or halting the breathing process but merely pausing during the point of transformation from inhalation to exhalation. This point of change is known as Ji (極), as in Taiji (太極) (Tai Chi) or the moment when Yin becomes Yang and vice versa. If we study the two moments of Ji in breathing, we see there are two distinct points of transformation (Ji) in the breath cycle. These two Ji are also a Yin and Yang pair and are integrally related opposites during a breath.

The moment of the Ji from exhalation to inhalation is the moment of transformation from Yin (inhalation) to Yang (exhalation), and so is the Ji moment that tonifies Yang or Fire in the body. The moment of the Ji from inhalation to exhalation is the moment of transformation (Ji) from Yang to Yin and so this moment tonifies Yin or Water in the body. This is the thinking found in the Ma Jia (馬家) (Ma Family) methods. Usually these moments of transformation are equal at both parts of the breath cycle, so the body remains balanced in breathing. Life goes on regularly. To build these elemental energies, we accentuate the Ji moment through a longer pause than is usual. To be clear, pausing at the end of exhale builds a fire (yang) and pausing at the end of inhalation builds Yin (water).

There are different methods for this type of Nei Gong (Qigong) determined by the goals of the practitioner. You can extend the pause at both points in equal amounts to cultivate both elements equally in the body. That is part of the practice in meditation. Or you can use this knowledge to cultivate one more than the other depending on the method. When training the fire-breathing Qigong discussed before, pause only at the fire point in the breath (after exhaling) to build a fire. In the following water Qigong, breathe at the water point (after inhaling) to produce water in the body. Ideally, this is done in equal parts to keep the practitioner healthy. Sometimes it can be used to help rebalance the body that is either too hot (fire) or too cold (water).

## Double Pause Breathing and Longevity (長壽)

Qi Ming, Chen (陳啟明), my Master in 18 Lo Han Palm (十八羅漢掌), is renowned for his work on longevity, having studied Taoist Immortality (道教成仙) practices and High-Level Buddhist Qigong (佛家氣功) over the past 50+ years. The following use of double pause breathing and an explanation of the Taoist point of view on longevity and breathing comes directly from him during my training.

Taoist philosophy has an ancient history going back thousands of years, and one of the many pursuits of Taoists is longevity. The Taoists of old worked from observing reality and studying what is real versus what we construct in our minds about reality. One of the realities of the world is that some animals live longer than others. By observing these animals and their lifespans things about how they lived their lives and used their bodies came to light. One of the animals most revered for their longevity is the Wu Gui (Tortoise) (烏龜) because they have life spans measured in the hundreds of years. Wu Gui became the ideal for a Taoist Zhen Ren or True Person (真人) on the path to Immortality (道教神仙).

One of the most important observations made by the past Masters of Taoism was that the quickness of the breath correlates to lifespan. Animals that breathe slowly live longer while animals that breathe quickly live shorter lives. For example, the lifespan of a dog is much quicker than a human lifespan and their breath reflects this. Rapid breathing increases the heart rate and the entire system runs more quickly, tiring out and degenerating swiftly. Another critical example is the lifespan of trees. They only breathe once a day, in for twelve hours and out for twelve hours and can live thousands of years. Now we see why so much Qigong is done near trees or have to do with trees.

According to studies done at the University of Rochester Medical Centre, the regular human respiratory rate at rest is 16-20 breaths per minute. The idea of Double pause breathing is to slow the respiration and force the body to become more efficient through training. The more efficient the body, the longer it lives, so the idea is that slow respiration increases longevity. This method slows the rate of breath to 4-6 per minute during practice. Pause at both the top of the breath (inhalation) and the bottom of the breath (exhalation). Be sure not to hold the breath. Instead, stop the breathing pattern at these points for a moment and then continue. It should be a seated meditation as a Nei Gong exercise for longevity. Training this daily for 100 days cause your natural breathing pattern to slow and the body to become more efficient. Shifu Chen has done a great deal of research on the arts of Taoist longevity and of all those methods, this is the foundation most overlooked and yet most important.

## 18 Lohan Palm Qi Regulation Method (十八蘆漢掌氣調節方法)

Begin seated in a comfortable position, ideally a half or full lotus position (全蓮花位置), with the legs crossed. Place the palms down on the knees while you settle the mind and breath. The palms are representative of the heart, and the heart and pericardium meridian are in the palm. The knees are representative of the kidneys. The connection of the palms and knees are a method of regulating the ferrying function of the heart and kidneys by balancing fire and water in the body.

After sitting a few minutes, open the hands and place them palm up on the knees. Now match the opening and closing of the hands with the inhalation and exhalation of the breath, using double pause breathing. During inhalation open the hands as the lungs open, and during exhalation close the fists. After practicing this for a time, turn the palms back over, settle the mind, and allow the breath to return to normal.

This practice is simple, but its depth is quite profound. When we are born our fists are clenched and we cling to life. When we perish our hands open and wrists turn outwards. This Qigong represents life and death in every breath and by balancing the heart and kidneys, it trains the body to be more efficient and breath more slowly. My Shifu has been practicing this Qigong for decades, and in his mid-70s many people are in awe of his black hair and strength when doing iron arms training. That's endorsement enough for me.

## Ma Family Water Breathing (馬家水氣功)

The counterpoint to the fire-breathing Qigong is this simple method that should be trained in equal or greater parts to the fire-breathing way. This method is not dangerous and can be practiced at any time for relief of stress, settling of the heart rate, or as a counterbalance to the fire Qigong. It cools the body and is a method of relieving excess fire from overtraining.

Stand with the feet shoulder width apart, the spine straight, and tongue touching the upper palate. Settle the mind and slow the breath. Imagine a silver bowl filled with cool water in front of Dantian. Place the hands in the bowl and bring them up the centre of the body as you inhale. Turn the palms towards the face and splash the water on the head, feeling the drips of cool water trickle down the front and back of the body during your exhalation. Slowly bring the hands down the centre of the body as you exhale and feel the coolness on your skin. Repeat 9, 18 or 36 times.

## Ma Family Iron-Body (馬家鐵體)

The Northern style I practice and teach descends from the Ma Family of Honan, a family-style based in old Shaolin training. The family had its unique method of training Iron-Body that falls in the Nei Gong (internal processes) school. By using the mind and the body without the external stimulus, the Ma Family created an Iron-Body Qigong with two levels- Iron-Body and Golden Bell Armor.

The first level of the training is essentially tricking the body through flexion of the torso. The movements are simple with the hands rising from the sides as you breathe in, rising above the shoulders before breathing out, then pressing the palms down the centre of the body towards the earth. This exhalation is done slowly and forcefully while you flex the entire torso save the peritoneal floor (Hui Yin) located between the anus and the genitals which acts a pressure release valve for the torso. It should merely relax, not flexed inwards OR outwards, or you run the risk of causing a hernia.

Warm up with three breaths with the arm movements and a relaxed body. Concentrate the mind on Dantian before your first breath of the Iron-Body practice. The abdominals, the back, neck, and pectorals (chest) should be flexed with all your strength on the first breath of Iron-Body training and held in tension as you raise your hands and intake your second breath. Although the torso is already flexed, you begin breathing out and flex again with all your strength. You essentially find muscle fibres that had not flexed on the first breath and cause them to activate. Continue this sequence with the torso flexed the entire time for up to eight breaths. On your final breath out, slow your breathing down as much as possible and press the palms downwards to the earth as though pushing down strong springs. Release the Qigong and your torso and cool down with three relaxed breaths with the same motion or Guan Qi Fa (Regulate the Qi Method).

## Ma Family Golden Bell Armor Qigong (馬家黄金鐘鎧甲氣功)

There are many types of Iron-Body training; some wholly external and others extremely internal in practice. The Ma Family Golden Bell Armor Qigong is one of the most esoteric Iron-Body Qigong I have come across. As with the other Ma Qigong, it involves visualization of fire in the body, and as such is dangerous. It is best to cool down after training with the water breathing Qigong or another similarly Yin method to avoid fire sickness.

Stand with the feet shoulder width in a high horse stance. Begin by settling the mind at Dantian and starting the fire-breathing method. As Dantian warms and becomes hot and the skin starts to open to the exterior (a gentle sweat) start the Golden Bell training.

As you inhale, bring the hands up above the head with the palms facing one another but not touching. In this posture visualize breathing through the hands to generate heat between the palms. When the hands have become hot, bring them down in front of Yin Tang. In this position continue to breathe fire in Dantian and out the palms of the hands. Feel the torso open to the exterior with a fine sweat.

Activate your nervous system through mental intention but without muscle flexion (Innervate) or imagine you are about to be struck on all sides of your torso. Imagine the surface of your skin becoming so hot as you exhale that any attacker would burn from touching you. On each exhalation, make the sound HA and exhale quickly. Expand the body in all directions by flexing the torso. Press the feet into the earth as you exhale, so the power forms in all directions including upwards and downwards. Innervate the expansion on inhalation and perform it on exhalation. Repeat nine times before bringing the hands down from Yintang to Tan Zhong (Centre of the chest) and repeat another nine times. Bring the hands down in front of Dantian with the fingers pointing at the earth and repeat another nine times.

When finished the sequence, release the palms from their position and bring the hands back up above the head and lower Qi to Dantian. Your palms face the earth and descend while the mind focuses on Dantian. Repeat three times.

After finishing the Qigong, I recommend training the water breathing Qigong as well as the Guan Qi Fa Qigong. This method is highly dangerous and is not recommended to be done without a qualified teacher. If you choose to train it, balance the fire in the body with water and cool yourself off. Be careful. I am writing to keep a record of these methods I learned, but they are also the methods that caused my run in with Qigong sickness. Stay vigilant in your training and pay attention to the warning signs of Qigong sickness.

# Heavy Hands Iron-Palm / Iron-Body Qigong (重手鐵體氣功)

Gu Yu Cheung's Heavy Hands Iron-Palm is possibly one of the best kept secret Iron-Palm methods in Chinese Martial Arts. Master Gu was incredibly famous as a Northern Shaolin Master who travelled to the South to teach, answering many challenges and never losing. He is shown in a well-known Iron-Palm photograph slapping through thirteen bricks without spacers, resting on the earth. There is even a documented account of him killing a horse with a single palm strike on the neck as it charged. He is the most famous exponent of Iron-Palm today and during his lifetime. But his methods, for some reason, are mainly unknown to the public. I was lucky enough to learn them from my Gongfu brother Professor Kevin Wallbridge, whose Teacher was a student of Northern Shaolin under one of Master Gu Yu Cheung's Disciples. Of all the Iron-Palm or Iron Fist methods I have studied, this system has given me the most remarkable results. It is also a safe Qigong to teach any time of the year although it is best if done in the fall and can be done daily without end.

The system is made up of the Heavy-hands Qigong, the light air exercises, and the five elements strike on the Iron-Palm bag.

## Heavy Hands Qigong (重手氣功)

### Taoist awaits the Dawn

Stand with the feet shoulder width apart and the body aligned for verticality by tucking the tailbone slightly and opening the neck as though listening backwards. Allow the hands to rest in their most natural state with the fingers falling as they may. Imagine a small ball under each armpit keeping this area open and free.

This entire Qigong is releasing tension from the body. We tend to hold ourselves back when striking by tightening muscle groups that are the antithesis to our movement so release becomes vital for the delivery of power. In Taoist awaits the Dawn release all tension you can find in the body from top to bottom as you prepare for the Qigong. Each posture in the Qigong should hold for eight to twelve slow and deep breaths.

## Immortal points the Way

Raise the arms out to shoulder height with your wrists slightly higher than elbows and level with shoulders. The arms should not make a 180-degree angle but should be slightly forward with the hands in your peripheral vision as you look ahead. The hands position as though the thumb and small finger were resting flat on a table top with the index finger highest and pointing outwards. The hands should be only slightly higher than the shoulders with index fingers turned upwards slightly.

Many of the positions have a line of intent within them, a place you should hold your mind while you are releasing and maintaining the position. Immortal points the way has a line of intent from the index finger up the inside of the forearm to the elbow that you should place your mind. It is the area you are training for striking.

## Heavy Hands

Return to the original position of Taoist awaits the Dawn. Change your mental intent behind the position. Feel the blood and lymph rushing back into the hands. It fills them and making them feel heavy. Merely experience and observe the sensation to this position.

## Penetrate the Mountain Passes

Settle the body slightly backwards as you raise the arms up until the elbows reach your ribs. Open the inside of the forearms to the sky (creating a positive spiral force Shun), then rotate the wrists inwards bringing the palms down to face the earth (forming a negative or counter flowing spiral force Ni). Reach the fingertips forward with the palm rounded.

The mind intent in Mountain Passes is the fingertips growing forward across the room to touch the opposite wall and the spine pulling backwards in a vertical line to equalize the forward intent and force. It will allow the body to settle downwards and backwards slightly to counterbalance the forward power. Mountain passes trains the ability to dot, Dian (點) with the fingertips into an opponent's body.

## Cradle the Celestial Embryo

Bring the arms back down the front of the body and round them as though you are holding a giant pregnant belly with your palms towards the underside of the abdomen and a small ball under each armpit. Settle deeply into the body and release as much tension as possible. The mind intent here is as if people were pressing inwards on your rounded arms trying to crush your belly and you are holding them off with outward pressure. Keep the roundness open and filled with potential but not physical strength. The main line of intent is from the middle finger along the outside of the forearms to the elbow. It trains backhanded forearm strikes found in many martial systems.

## Open the Window to Look at the Moon

Sink 2 inches keeping the spine straight and maintaining verticality while releasing as much tension as possible throughout your body. Bring the hands up and in front of the head as though holding something above you with the knife edges of your hands. The eyes should look up and forward between the fingers without changing the heads verticality. Look up only with your eyes and do not change the neck. Settle the tailbone downwards while pressing gently upwards with the hands creating traction in the spine. The line of intent in Open the Window to look at the Moon is from the end of the pinky finger through to the wrist, the knife edge of the hand.

## Great Solar Stance

Bring the hands down in front of the body as though you were holding a beach ball on your chest with the palms facing the body. It is like the standard Zhan Zhuang posture, but with a different mindset involved. Instead of working for only relaxation, the mentality here is explained by the poetry of the posture. "Imagine you are holding the sun on your chest, it is expanding in all directions, and you are holding it inwards and keeping it on your chest." As well as the saying "Melt the snow all around you from the heat of your body." Heat is dangerous, so it is alright to feel the warmth of this posture and the next but always remember the saying for heavy hands Qigong "The bones are light and cool, and the flesh is heavy and wet." Be sure the body cools after the postures are finished. Do not seek to continue with the feeling of warmth. The posture trains strikes that come back towards the body with the palms of the hands.

## Fire Palms

Settle into your legs and drop your stance straight down another four inches while bringing your arms down from the great solar stance. Place the elbows on the ribs and pull back the fingers while the heels of the palms press forward, and the palms opened. The mind here follows the instruction "The fire in your legs fans the flames in your palms." Press the feet downwards into the earth and allow the upward pressure to line directly from the feet to the palms so pressing downwards presses the palms forward. The legs should burn from the depth of the stance during this posture. It trains forward palm heel strikes.

## Bear down like Tai Shan (Great Mountain)

Stand up to the natural stance from the beginning of the set and lift the arms up the centre of the body. As you reach the top of the new stance, bring the arms from above your head down and out in sight of your peripheral vision to the sides of your shoulders. Be sure the arms stay at that level with the elbows pointing downwards and the wrists and hands slightly higher than the shoulders. Bear down like Tai Shan trains the Arm like a sword strikes and the mindset in this posture is that your arms are on a tabletop and you are allowing your heavy arms to work to drop through the tabletop on which they are resting. The hands should hold naturally but in a knife hand shape (Pi Zhang Splitting palm) as though you were executing the strike.

## Pillar of Heaven

Bring the hands back up over the head like the posture Open the Window to look at the Moon but instead of the hands held like a knife open the palms and press them upwards towards heaven. The eyes look forward as well in this posture.

This posture is the first of the two internal Iron-Body methods in Heavy Hands Qigong. The mindset is preparing yourself to be struck from the front with a board or staff. It means you are not tightening the front of the iron vest but are prepared. Ideally, this is the act of innervation. Use the mind to activate the nervous system and bringing the body to the point about to flex the torso to protect itself but hold back from the action. If done with a great deal of mind intent, the feeling in the torso sometimes resembles tingling, electricity, or heat. It is known as the Qi feeling traditionally, and as Qi is a relationship, it is the feeling of a powerful connection between the mind and body, Shen and Jing (神精).

## Spiritual Tortoise

The fingers turn upwards, and the hands are brought down the centre of the body to just below the solar plexus. Keep the fingers pointing upwards and the palms facing one another. Round the back slightly as though you were about to be struck from behind by an opponent by a board or stick. It is the same as the Pillar of Heaven posture, and you innervate the flexion of the back of the Iron Vest.

## Taoist awaits the Dawn

Return to the first posture of the set and allow your hands to fall into their natural relationship to your elbow. Allow your body to sort out what it is feeling and naturalize to what the Qigong has done, feel what you feel and if it is nothing that's alright too. Spend the eight to twelve breaths relaxing and experiencing the end of the Qigong.

## Light Air Exercises

These exercises are another of the rarely shared aspects of this system and are essential in the integration of the whole to achieve Iron-Palm. They should be done directly after finishing the Qigong, so the feeling of heaviness is present in the hands and arms to give you the sensory experience of moving martially with the heavy feel.
Each exercise should be done at least 36 times but ideally more, be sure to train each side equally.

Stand in Ma Bu (Horse stance). Bring both palms downwards as though slapping them on a table and allow the forearms to strike the thighs on each strike. Turn the hands over and bring them down as though hitting with the back of the hands. These are done quickly but relaxed and with a lot of heaviness.

Stand in Gong Bu (Bow and Arrow Stance). Rotate the hands for these strikes in the air. The lead hand starts with the back of the hand strikes at head height, and the rear hand will turn and palm strike downwards towards the floor. Repeat for the other side.

Stay in Gong Bu (Bow and Arrow Stance). The next attack is knife edge of the hand forwards at head height. The rear hand continues to rotate and palm strike towards the floor. Repeat for the other side.

Remain in Gong Bu (Bow and Arrow Stance). The last attack is a back-fist with the lead hand while the rear hand rotates, and palm strikes towards the floor.

## Five Elements Iron-Palm Bag Work (五行铁沙掌)

This is the most common type of Iron-Palm training and is more widely seen. The five elements refer to the kind of power, Jin (劲) that you are working to generate. In each strike is a type of Jin that you should be working to produce and the method of dropping the hand must be followed to gain the benefit of the bag work.

Earth (土) is the first palm strike done in the sequence and is most associated with Iron-Palm training. Drop the centre of the palm flat onto the bag with a soft, even power. The Jin of Earth is even and should descend through the bag to the floor in a horizontal, even wave. It is difficult to describe in text what power or Jin feels like but one way to look at earth Jin is like a descending line of force like the = symbol. Strike from the top of the bag and it descends equally through the target.

Water (水) is the second strike of the sequence and is done with the back of the hand. After striking with the earth palm turn the hand and drop it in a round shape on the back of the palm. Be sure to keep the fingers from hitting the bag. The surface for striking is the back of the hand only. The water palm is known by its effect on the back. When you strike the centre of your bag, the edges should 'splash' upwards as though your hand had hit water itself instead of beans. It is a round, curved power that penetrates in a smaller surface area than earth palm and has the shape like a cup as it drops through the bag.

Wood (木) is the third of the strikes in the sequence and is the knife edge or chopping edge of the hand. With the hand thumb up, keep the fingers together so they do not strike one another, which can result in damage to the fingers, and drop the knife edge of the hand through the bag as though you were cutting a deep trench in it. If the bag is struck correctly, it will take on the shape of the trench I am mentioning when you remove your hand. Wood palm is the Jin of cutting and crushing. The power cuts deeply into the bag as though cleaving something in two.

Fire (火) is the fourth strike of the sequence and has a more complicated method. Still drop the hand heavily into the bag by releasing the joints, but just before the moment of impact you 'pop' the palm heel into the bag for the strike. This method will burst the power forward through the bag from the long bones (radius and ulna) of the arm and the beans will move towards the far end of the bag each strike. The Jin of fire bursts from the centre and penetrates the body of the opponent like an expanding bullet. The heaviness of the hand coupled with the sudden burst of the palm at the moment of impact will create the expanding penetrating feeling in the body of the person struck.

Metal (金) is the final strike and is known as 'dotting' the bag. This is not done by all practitioners due to the level of complexity and pain involved in making mistakes. This strike conditions the fingertips and allows them to transfer spiral force through a tiny surface area. Each of the five digits must hit the bag at the same time and the hand shape is crucial to avoid damaging yourself. The hand should be held with the digits all able to strike at once and the palm cupped into a round shape to support the fingers with the bones of the hand (metacarpals). Spiral the entire hand from the wrist inwards, so the thumb is moving towards your torso as you strike. This not only creates the penetrating spiral force (the dotting Jin) but also distributes the power evenly through the digits and hand to avoid damage. Of course, you need to be careful when training this strike, and it will be done with less force than the others until the hand is conditioned. Avoiding injuries from training is of the utmost importance!

With all five strikes in a row, I tend to change from hand to hand after a predetermined number to keep things even and equal in the training. Progress slowly and with care to avoid arthritis later in life.

## The Bag (鐵沙掌袋)

The bag itself should be bigger than your outstretched hand to avoid hitting the surface underneath. In many traditions, like the external Iron-Palm I learned when young, you change the interior of the bag over time from mung beans to sand to gravel to iron or steel shot and sometimes even progressing until you are just slapping a rock! When I was in my early twenties, I went to a stone tombstone shop and bought a piece of broken granite tombstone to use. It was not the most fun thing I have ever trained.

In this Internal method, only a bag filled with beans is used. It is not changed to harder materials. This type of training is about the release of joints and not about the material you hit. It is not so much 'hand conditioning' as a release of tension throughout the joints to allow your generated heaviness to drop through your hands. Any bag will do. Fill it with enough beans to avoid striking through them and hitting the surface below. Traditionally, mung beans are used because they have medicinal properties for healing bones. However, this only works if the dust from the beans as they are crushed can get through the material of the bag and onto your hands. If you do not have this kind of material, then the type of beans becomes moot. I have mung in my bag while one of my Gongfu brothers is using lentils. Either way, if you are ever in trouble you should be able to make soup.

The use of Dit Da Jow is mentioned previously. For the training of Iron-Palm it is essential to heal fast enough to avoid real long-term damage to the hands. An excellent herbal liniment will help heal after each session. If you cannot make or order either of the recipes in this book, you may be able to find some commercially available ones online that will work as well.

## Releasing the Joints

Releasing the joints is the essential part of the bag work in the internal Iron-Palm method and consists of three levels of training. Releasing the joints refers to removing all tension from the muscularity around a joint or series of joints to allow the limb to fall through the bag when training. The idea is deceptively simple, but not easy. When we extend our arm to strike someone, the triceps muscle fires and contracts to lengthen the arm and create force. Commonly this clenches the bicep at the same time essentially slowing down the arm but feeling the opposing forces and the power they are generating. This is like driving a car with the brake pedal to the floor. It may still move forward but not at its most efficient.

When we strike, we need to release the muscularity that is in opposition to the movement of the strike itself and stop slowing ourselves down in the transfer of force. To gain the heavy hands from this training we need to release tension from the body while we strike to teach our brains and nervous systems to activate in the desired way instinctively. So, we practice joint release on the bag to have the stimulus of striking an object while releasing joints.

## Drunken Style Cotton Belly (醉拳棉肚)

One of the true skills of Drunken Boxing, Cotton Belly is the reason a skilled drunken boxer can allow an opponent to strike them, remain unhurt, and turn that power into attacking momentum.

When receiving a strike to the body, using Cotton Belly does not mean you are so relaxed that there is no muscular contraction to protect the internal organs. While it may appear that way to the outside observer, the drunken player does have a muscular contraction to armour the body but remains soft enough to move and be moved by the incoming force. It is because of this balance and counter-intuitive approach that Cotton Belly tends to be challenging to learn and takes some time training with a partner to gain the skill. It is a real balance of Yin Yang tension in the body to be able to take significant amounts of force without damage and retain all your mobility.

Stand with the feet shoulder width apart and identify that you are about to be hit and ready yourself to tighten the torso but do not tighten it yet or fully. Have your partner hit you in the stomach off centre to the left or right. Allow the force to fold your body and move the leg under the strike. So, if the right side of your torso is truck, your right leg moves back as the body turns and deflects the remaining force. Once this becomes easy, work on the upper torso with soft strikes to the chest. Remember to move the legs to absorb and deflect the force. Once this can be done quickly with full force strikes, progress to the next stage of training.

### Turning from Chong Mai (Axular Movement)

In front of the spine is the vertical centre of the body. In TCM it can be referred to as Chong Mai or the Penetrative Vessel, a vestigial meridian from our evolution. In Drunken boxing, the entire connecting Axular line from Hui Yin (perineum) to Bai Hui (top of the head) is Chong Mai.

When using Cotton Belly to absorb and deflect force, you should always turn from Chong Mai to the left or right. When your partner strikes you dead centre and gives neither left nor right direction to the force, it is up to you to decide which direction to take it. Turning from this central axle allows you to absorb and turn the force away from your internal organs and create force back towards the opponent from your opposite side. For example, if the partner strikes your right side, you step back with your right foot, turn on Chong Mai, and deliver their power back to them with your left hand. It will protect you from damage, allow you to use their power against them, as well as add your acceleration to it just before the strike. Once you can deliver power back at the partner as a result of their strike you are ready for the next stage of training.

## Turning from Dantian

Turning from Dantian adds three-dimensional movement to the already deep central movement of the body from Chong Mai. Instead of just left and right this adds bending forward and back from the waist and back as well. Chong Mai runs vertically through the body and the Belt Meridian. Dai Mai runs around the waist like a belt. The intersection of these two meridians becomes the physical centre of the body and is Dantian.

When your partner strikes, allow the movement to lean you back or forward as well as turn you left or right. Chong Mai remains your axle for left and right power while Dantian becomes your centre point for back and forward. A great many of the Drunken postures like Rapid Wind and Strong Grass and Protect the Family Fist lean and bend in this way and are examples of three-dimensional movement from Dantian. When done correctly it should not matter what part of the body is struck or at what angle. You should be able to turn, lean, absorb and deliver power back to the opponent from their acceleration of your body. To train this, have your partner strike softly at any part of your body, front or back, and allow it to move you and turn you and retaliate. When this becomes easier, you are ready for the last level of training.

Blindfold yourself. Train with a partner you trust and who is ready to deal with your attacks back at them. Let them strike you softly without any announcement until you can feel and execute Cotton Belly without any optical or sonic warning. It is a high-level skill and takes time, so go slowly. Once Cotton Belly starts to work, attack your opponent using the seven stars of attack. The Seven stars are the striking points on the body which are hand, elbow, shoulder, hips, knees, feet, and side of the head.

Both left and right means 14 striking points. The saying "Whole body is a fist" comes into play here. You should be training all the parts of the body to deliver power just like the seated section of our second drunken form where we train Kao Jin (Body Attack Power) by striking with the shoulders and shoulder blades. Remember the most critical part of Drunken Boxing is the use of the Three spheres of combat. Take control of the opponent's body and the central space between you while giving up control of your own. Allowing yourself to be pushed around and manipulated by the opponent's power. Blocking a strike from the opponent will set off the Cotton Belly training and move you to absorb and use the opponent's force against them.

The appearance of skill in Drunken Boxing is easy to fake. But it is the touch of the Drunken Boxer that will tell the truth. Their ability to absorb, deflect, and redirect incoming force is the real mark of the style. When I am teaching or meeting other Drunken Boxers, Cotton Belly is the skill I test to see a person's skill level. It is challenging to let go in this way, and it requires a lot of time spent training. Do not get frustrated. It took me nearly seven years before my Drunken stopped just appearing to be the real thing and instead started to act the way Cotton Belly training should make it.

# Yi Jin Jing (易筋经)

Master-Professor Kevin Wallbridge is my Gongfu brother and was the person who taught me the Yi Jin Jing. It is relatively rare to have any real understanding of the set and how to train for the most results. Many thanks to Kevin for taking the time to share this info and answer the questions of students so openly.

Yi Jin Jing (易筋经) translates to Muscle-Tendon Change. Yì (易) is an old character that shows rays of the sun. We know from experience that the sun's rays cause great transformations, drying, tanning, ripening, etc. Jin (筋) has bamboo above, flesh on the left, and strength on the right. It means the flesh that has the strength of bamboo. We call this contractile tissue. It is much more than muscle, which is just meat. It is tendons, ligaments and the fascial network. Jing (经) refers to things that are long like rivers. Here it means the meridian system. So, Muscle-tendon Change may also be rendered the method to transform the fascia network.

It is a Yingong (硬功) or hard Qigong and comes with obvious physical risks. The process involves strong muscular contractions, both isotonic (moving under tension) and isometric (static under tension). It can lead to dramatic increases in abdominal pressure which can cause hernias or arterial aneurysms. If the alignments of the joints are incorrect, it can lead to structural problems, especially the neck or shoulders. It is possible to rupture a vertebral disc in the neck or a bursa in the shoulder. From a Chinese medicine perspective, if the breathing is incorrect, you can hobble the Qi mechanism and cause kidney exhaustion and thermal problems like night sweats or tidal fevers.

The method begins with reverse breathing. Reverse breathing involves drawing Dantian towards Ming-men on the inhalation.

It closes the lower abdomen while the diaphragm opens in the middle. So lower belly in and upper belly out on inhaling. As well, the perineal floor (between the anus and genitals) picks up as you inhale. The lower body rolls in a circle as you breathe; in and upon inhalation and out and down on exhalation. It is a method that is worth practicing until it is natural. Just doing reverse breathing is a hugely important meditation in Daoist internal work.

When practicing the shapes, you are contracting most of the body but the lower belly and especially the floor of the pelvis are releasing. It is essential for stabilizing the internal abdominal pressure. As you move, there is double-pause breathing (at the top and the bottom of the breath). At the top of the inhalation, you pause the breath (don't hold it or seal it) and begin the contraction. At the bottom of the breath you pause and release the rib cage (core) before you release the limbs (periphery).

If you have a version of the form already slowly try to apply this breathing pattern to it. It improves the transformative quality of the form. Reverse breathing is worth practicing for three years all on its own.

## Reverse (Taoist) Breathing and Belly (Buddhist) Breathing

Since the Yi Jin Jing requires lots of effort we are breathing quite profoundly. There is no resting and each breath is a contraction so being aware of the pausing as opposed to sealing the breath is important.

When we breathe deeply, the rib cage lifts and the neck muscles become engaged. At the top of a large breath, the deep erectors of the lower back also engage to tilt the ribs upward in front. When you stop inhaling a deep breath the instinct is to release the lower back and allow the ribs to lean forward to a neutral position. However, at this point, if you try to exhale it is like forcing your way through a mostly closed door (sealing the breath). What typically happens is the back will re-engage and lift the breast-bone then the exhalation gasps out. In the Yi Jin Jing we want to keep the ribs tilted at the top when we pause the inhale, so we can start exhaling without having to lift the breast-bone again.

In Daoist practice, we call belly breathing Buddhist breathing, and consider reverse-breathing to be the norm for Nei Gong. References to Taīxī (胎息) or embryonic-breathing go back to the period before the introduction of Buddhism into China, so it may be that belly-breathing came from India with Buddhism. Reverse-breathing strengthens the flow through the Ren and Du meridians (任督经脉). What some call Xiaǒzhoūtiañ (小周天) or small heavenly orbit. The connection between the Dantian and Ming-men allows the acquired constitution to sustain the innate constitution and the natural constitution to inspire the acquired constitution. This is good for long life.

Consider the role of the breath in the expression of power. When we hit, the most common coordination is to exhale as we express the Fa Jin(发劲). When we do reverse breathing, we can combine soft and hard in the hit because the perineal floor is releasing while the body is engaging. The nature of the force changes. The whole body hitting with the pelvic floor engaged can give crisp quality to the hit. It is useful where the opponent is tentative or cautious (what I like to call a 'muffin'). However, if the opponent is braced and hard, these kinds of hits often impact against the surface. It can take many many hits to wear your way through. If the pelvic floor can release while the body and significant joints engage for the hit, there is another quality to the power. There is still a bang that can disrupt the weaker structures but there is something else as well. There is a deadening follow-through that can penetrate deeply into the opponent's tissues. It can disrupt joints or bruise down to the bone when hitting limbs. On the torso or head, the force washes through the interior like a tidal wave, smashing anything in its path. These are not the only ways of generating these Jin, but it can be a place to start.

The application of breath during inhalation and exhalation for throwing and lifting techniques is important as well. It is done a great deal in Taiji and can be used in any martial art once it is understood. The secret sounds of Chen Taiji are 'heng' (The sound of a quick inhalation) and 'ha' (the sound of a quick exhalation).

But the idea of inhalation and exhalation is not always clear. In this case, what we are doing is not so much 'inhaling' or 'exhaling' but instead contracting the intercostal muscles to either breathe in or out. So, it is not so much 'breath control' as it is torso control. Use the musculature of the breathing apparatus to force air either in or out of the lungs rather than by breathing as you usually do. It engages more muscularity and does so on purpose, allowing us to recruit this contraction to create power.

## Torso Control

At first, hold it more staccato in tempo and keep each piece clear. It can become smoother as your skill level progresses. The torso must release before the breath releases otherwise you can set up down-bearing in the body. Breath release first may seem easier but in the long run, it can lead to problems. Release the centre of the chest first before you let the perineal/pelvic floor go. It is one reason that I advocate a more broken approach, these pieces shouldn't be too blurred, or you set up issues for later. Hard Qigong is dangerous, and not always in the obvious ways.

Focus on the source of the breath impulse. Practice ten to twelve nice slow reverse breaths while you are lying on your back in a comfortable, supported position with something under your neck and something under your knees. Once you are relaxed and the reverse breathing is a smooth exhalation, pause at the bottom and wait. Pay attention to the place in your chest from where the impulse to inhale comes. That place is where the body needs to relax towards at the end of the contractions in the Yi Jin Jing. That spot is where you want the downhill grade of relaxation out of the limbs to be heading when the breath lets go. It needs to be going there first before the breath releases.

# Martial Ramblings

by Sifu Neil Ripski

# Combat in a Marketplace

A Backpack and Sword is all I brought with me to Nepal. I packed up everything I owned, including my entire Martial Arts School, and put it in storage while I headed out there to take a walk. Within the first ten days I had already taught classes of martial arts to hundreds of students, private lessons to the advanced players of World United Martial Arts Association and even had the chance to use my Gongfu in the marketplace.

It was interesting when the beggar grabbed me, asking for a handout. He was obviously out of his mind and reeked of the local whisky. Grabbing my arm and pulling me towards him I could feel the intention he had to try and affect my mind with his actions. No violence took place, of course, I slowly swatted his hand off of me and looked into his eyes while I told him not to touch me again. My intent was clear. He backed off reluctantly, and it reminded me of the pickpocket in Rome the previous year. An excellent moment for training, to meet mind to mind with him and be in the moment together.

There are of course legends and fictional stories about Masters and Warriors meeting in mind to mind combat, locking in battle together only mentally and determining the winner. It is usually played up as a fight scene in movies or stories that takes place in a mysterious way where both opponents can see the outcome in their minds. The reality is much more mundane, as it always is with legends, but that does not mean it is any less real. He and I both had a moment in time where together we measured the intent and possible outcome of a conflict. So, what happened? What is the mind to mind combat in real life, without the fantasy?

Meeting eyes with someone for the first time, at a party let us say, is no different. If there is a strong attraction, that feeling is palpable to you and your body language, physical response

by Sifu Neil Ripski

(pheromones), and movements send a message to the other person. Communication without words is a part of being human and we all do it without thinking about it. Many of our first impressions of one another come from this kind of gathering of information. Martial Artists who are training to break through the barriers of mediocrity should be studying this. The art is about studying the self and humanity. We are more similar than different and experiences like this occur in everyone's life. The differences between the external fighter and the internal cultivator are many. Looking more deeply at the non-verbal interactions we all have as human beings is one of the more profound differences and can result a great deal of self-improvement as well as higher levels of skill when it comes back to martial use and application.

Communication is the key here, talking without words can be powerful. More so than words in many cases. In Chinese martial arts and medicine, we could use the classical language stating that the Zhi (mind intent or willpower) can affect the reactions of your body to your thoughts. The traditional saying Yi Ling Qi or the Mind leads the Qi means the same thing. In the case of interactions with others, we can say that my Qi as a relationship within my body because my thoughts effect reaction within me that can affect others and their reactions and relationships to me. Some people appear to be approachable. Others do not. Some people can be seen or felt to be in a bad mood while others give us the impression, they are open and friendly. In the case of potential violence, the tension we feel is another example. That moment and feeling can be trained as a skill. Are we afraid of the outcome of the next moment or not? What are our intentions for the next moment? These affect the result of the next moment for our opponent and ourselves profoundly.

To train our ability at that moment in between thought and action we first need to look at how we define Qigong and Nei Gong. Qigong we define as the work of studying relationships which can mean anything from the relationships in the muscularity around the joints of the body to your relationship as a human being to the world around you. Nei Gong means inner or inside work and is the work of studying the relationships within yourself. Your ties to fear or anger, your link to the concept of death (the existential crisis), or your connection to stimuli from outside the body and how it affects your emotions are all Nei Gong. To quote my Gongfu brother Kevin "Qigong corrects flaws in your structure, Nei Gong is to correct flaws in your character."

An example of an exercise here would be Deer Nei Gong. When done physically, it is called a Qigong in the Five Animal Frolics and involves turning the head and spine and opening the neck while looking behind. But when practiced as a Nei Gong, it is quite different. The Deer is a prey animal and as such always needs to be aware of predators. The Nei Gong portion of the exercise is to stop moving and straighten the spine looking forwards while listening backwards. Essentially invoke the feeling that you are walking in the forest and hear something behind you, something that could be a predator stalking you, ready to end your life. It is a feeling of aliveness, caution and fear, invigorating the kidneys and nervous system alike. The slow and deliberate turn to look behind allows you to stay in the moment and experience the feeling of the flight or fight response about to take place. Once you have looked over your shoulder behind yourself and you believe nothing is there, a conscious and complete reaction takes place disengaging the response and returning you to normal. Take a moment in time usually wholly overlooked and instinctive, slow it down and study it, feel it and your reaction to it both mentally and emotionally. That is Nei Gong. The moment before impending violence is no different than this, we can all feel it but few studies it.

Looking into the man's eyes after I removed his hand, we both experienced this moment of fight or flight. I could feel his intent was predatory, not prey, and as such my instincts were in the moment before fight or flight as well. To act as prey would probably invite violence in this case so instead, I chose to be a predator as well, ideally the bigger one. Without fear or remorse, I softened my joints and opened my back and neck and told him firmly not to touch me again. That moment was the combat of the minds where our body language and mind intent clashed, and we both made decisions. He backed away, and I relaxed and carried on through the market. No one was the wiser among the people around us what took place. Every single moment is an opportunity to train. It is up to us to recognize them and take advantage of them. Do not waste them.

# Opening the Small Gates of Baguazhang

The Bagua Small Gate Opening Palm, Ba Gua Xiao Kai Men Zhang (八卦小門開掌) is a short form of Baguazhang that I teach to all my serious students. The name Xiao Kai Men Zhang is always the first thing I am asked about. What are the gates? This depends on context as is usual in Chinese Arts and Language. From a health or Qigong standpoint, the small gates are the joints of the body. Opening these gates means to soften, stretch, and make pliable each one of your joints. They are Ankle, Knee, Hip, Wrist, Elbow, Shoulder, Dantian (Kua), Tan Zhong (Chest), Neck (Da Zhui), and Mind (Upper Dantian).

The first six (twelve if you count both sides) of these joints must be relaxed and have equal amounts of muscular tension around them to be opened. It is physically difficult because as overly strong or weak muscle groups tend to unbalance the strength around a joint. For example, overdeveloped quadriceps (thigh muscle) can overpower the muscularity in the lower leg and therefore pull on the knee joint more in one direction than another. Ideally training the small gate form will allow the quad to relax while the lower leg bears more of the strain of movement and allows it to grow stronger to balance the tension around the knee joint. Each of these Six Harmonies (12 joints) work in this way and should be studied to make them all relaxed, even, smooth, and open.

The Kua involves more than the hip joint as it includes the entire muscularity of the inguinal crease joint and all the attachments in the pelvis. Dantian is another way of looking at this. Equally working the six directions of Dantian through three-dimensional movement will help all the Kua muscles and abdominal muscularity to become active and ideally balanced for any action. It means that any movement in any angle starting from the Dantian should have equal substance, force, and stability. Cultivating the six directions of Dantian can be done through this form

by Sifu Neil Ripski

although there are other more specific exercises for it as well.

Developing Tan Zhong (Middle Dantian) for movement is one of the particularly focused skills within Baguazhang. Tan Zhong should be able to move in any direction independently of the lower Dantian and have equal muscular tension on both sides. It is a gate of the body that is difficult to open, and as such there are other Bagua exercises designed to work on it more directly than Xiao Kai Men Zhang. The Eight Small Palms of Cheng Style Bagua (八小掌), seated Fu Zhu Gong Fa exercises, and many drills have been developed to work this area more directly. In Xiao Kai Men Zhang it is a part of the training to work Tan Zhong, especially in movements such as White Snake Coils the Body or Remove the Helmet from Behind. It is an essential part of Bagua training and its health benefits include internal organ massage through movement and washing the organs with blood.

Da Zhui (Neck) is overlooked in many martial arts. In this form, the most visible work on the neck is within Dragon Rolls the Ball at the opening of the form. By rotating the hands to play with the ball using Tan Zhong, the torso moves back and forth a great deal. If the neck remains relaxed and eyes gaze straight ahead, the torso will move while the head stays still, stretching and moving the neck to keep the head in place. For the neck to open correctly, it must be relaxed and extended from the base (Da Zhui) to the top of the neck at the bottom of the skull (Feng Fu). The muscularity of the neck starts under the skull and extends down under the scapula (shoulder blades). Again, a particular exercise exists for each of the three joints on the centre of the body, Dantian, Tan Zhong, and the Neck known as Six Balls & One Pillar Exercises. Xiao Kai Men Zhang does some work on the neck mainly through keeping the gaze and head still and through obeying the saying "Look Forward and listen backwards" or open the neck, pull up the back of the head, and tuck the chin.

The final joint is the Upper Dantian, Shang Dantian (上丹田) or the mind. The location of the upper Dantian is thought to be in the centre of the head. The mind is a big topic in internal training and involves the Shen (Spirit) and Yi (Intention & Intellect). To open the gate of the upper Dantian in Xiao Kai Men Zhang bring the mind entirely to focus on the form itself. Become soft in intention and relaxed in intent. Remain undistracted by other thoughts as you observe the small joints of the body and the requirements to open and relax each one. The mind becomes one-pointed and enters a state of meditation. Calm the monkey mind that likes to jump from one thing to another and keep it still and focused on the task at hand. Xiao Kai Men Zhang is an excellent form for this moving meditation as it is brief, has a right amount of depth and detail in its movements, and allowing the mind to enter a state of meditation in this way has many health benefits.

The human immune system is taxed a great deal by stress from depression or anxiety, living in the past or future rather than the present. Becoming centred on the present moment even for a short while during practice allows the immune system a small rest from the stress of trying to exist in any state other than the present. If you focus on the here and now, the worries of the rest of life fall away and the stress along with it, even if it is only for a moment. The Mind is the most important gate to relax and make smooth. Focused and robust, the mind leads the body to a state closer to balance.

Combatively the small gates can also to opening the opponent's gates as well. These are the nine gates of the body where techniques can infiltrate the opponent's defense. They are Left, Middle, Right, Upper, Middle, Lower gates for a nine-position grid. Or they can refer to changing the structure, power, and balance around the opponent's joints (Ankle, Knee, Hip, Wrist, Elbow, Shoulder, Dantian, Tan Zhong, Da Zhui, Upper Dantian). Balance is the state we are trying to achieve in training and harmonizing with the opponent is a high-level skill. Being able to change the balance around an opponent's joint, physical or mental, changes the way their body, mind, and nervous system will respond to you in combat. Understanding how to balance and open your joints teaches you its opposite, how to close or unbalance an opponent.

Any form that is worth learning has a depth that is not always readily apparent. Each form is like a carrier of a style's DNA. Just because DNA passes on it does not mean that those who receive it always realize its potential. If your family genes tend to have great musical ability you still need tenacious hard work, practice, and memorization to become a great musician. A great style, great form, and even a great teacher will never be enough to create greatness in a student. Realizing the potential of learning a form comes from in-depth study, introspection and testing. Without a ton of time and hard work, Gongfu (功夫), even the best style can be wasted on lazy students.

Bagua is hard, man.

# On Teaching Martial Arts

Teaching Martial Arts is a big responsibility to take on. Shaping a new generation of students and keeping a style alive by passing it on is no small thing. Without real understanding and perspective our styles, it is easy to pass on pure rhetoric rather than a living breathing art. It is the depth of understanding and context of the system and its skills while teaching that separates a martial arts instructor from a real master teacher.

Perspective is the first part of the formula. The longer we train and further into the depth of the art we get, the better our perspective becomes when teaching students. For example, if a teacher has been training for five years and recently become an instructor, they have only begun to cultivate higher level skills. As such, they do not yet have the perspective to see how teaching of the art is organized. They are still going through the process of growth and cultivation themselves. It can be argued that the process of cultivation and growth never stops, which is true, but the long-term effects of training can only be seen from where the teacher stands. The view from five years deep into practice is entirely different from thirty years deep.

To have a real understanding and broad perspective on teaching others, it is important to have both a breadth of knowledge as well as a reasonable depth of experience in the subjects. In the Chinese Martial Arts, for example, breadth of education for a teacher should include an understanding of Chinese Culture, History, Language, Medicine, Philosophy, Writing, and Fighting skills. We do not need to be experts in every field listed here, but the depth of knowledge in each of these areas will overlap to make understanding the Chinese martial arts deeper and broader, thus making the person who has this knowledge a better teacher with a broader perspective.

Looking at fighting skills of Chinese Martial Arts alone, we can break the art down into many different parts and aspects of training that we should know. The four elements of Chinese martial arts include Ti (Kicking), Da (Striking or hitting), Shuai (Throwing), and Na (Seizing). Each of these four aspects can be broken down further to find more depth of knowledge. For example, Qin Na (Grasping and Seizing Control) has four elements: Tearing Tendons & Breaking bones, Sealing the Blood, Sealing the Breath, and Attacking Acupoints. Understanding applications of the arts can be seen in four aspects as well.

Level One is the obvious application of a movement.

Level Two is the application of the movement but changing the attack or direction of the attack from the opponent. A right-handed punch becomes a grab from the side or behind. See how we use the same movement to affect the opponent.

Level Three asks what aspect is missing? Use the first two levels to find what aspect of the movement has not been explored. For example, a hand technique applied on the first two levels is most likely overlooking the role of the stance, steps and legs. The same hand technique may cut the stance, destroying the opponent's balance, attacking the joints or have outright kicking applications hidden beneath the upper body during the movement.

Level Four develops better, more precise targeting. If a hand technique is being applied and striking the head of the opponent, what specific targeting could be used to have more effect on the opponent? There is a difference between driving a punch into the opponent's head and taking a more exact approach and striking an acupoint for a more dramatic effect. Some examples of this may be Jian Jing (Shoulder well gb21) rather than just the head. Jian Jing is one of the most down bearing points in the body, and a heavy strike here will buckle the knees of the opponent. Another example may be Tai Yang (Greater Yang ex3) located on the temple of the head, which a massive strike can concuss the brain itself and cause swelling and a great deal of damage with a transfer of real power.

From a teaching perspective of a single technique, whether it is an application, or a movement pulled from a form, we can pass on many answers to the question "Why?" from the student. If we have multiple ways of thinking, depths of understanding, levels of damage, and application for each movement. An even better way of sharing is teaching students these ways of thought so that they can disassemble and investigate their art on their own. That teaches critical thinking and methods of application they can use themselves.

Cultural context, language, philosophy, and history play essential roles in the understanding of the arts. They each give us a background to look at the art we are studying and not only how things are done or described, but why they are. An old martial saying states "Do not seek to be like the men of old, seek what they sought." It is this that changes the perspective of a student learning an art. It is not enough to learn the movements, forms, and weapons of an art from a famous master. We must try to understand what it was that master, that icon we are emulating, was working on. That way we can understand what made them gain the high levels of skill for which they became famous. Understanding how the Chinese were affected by their language and philosophies and thus their thought processes gives us an approximate understanding of what the originators were thinking.

A good example is the native philosophy of Taoism from China. From there comes the idea of Taiji (太極 Great Ultimate). The study and understanding of the points of transformation from Yin to Yang when studying aspects of anything is all permeating to a certain extent in the martial arts. Each movement is executed in a way that demonstrates the tremendous Ultimate idea, showing each aspect of Yin and Yang and the transformation between them. To describe it on a more modern fundamental level, every action has an equal and opposite reaction. For every part of the body moving forward, another part must move backwards, and so on. In any single movement, there are multiple examples of the Yin and Yang reversal in the body. Understanding and studying this will allow the martial arts teacher to see more deeply into their techniques and as such help their students to balance and harmonize the movement of their bodies. It is a rough and basic look into the topic of Yin and Yang reversal but demonstrates the thought model you can use based on Taoist philosophy for deepening understanding of martial movement.

The deeper you go into each of these subjects; the more you can see its influence on the arts already and allow us to have a guideline to correct our movements.

Language influences how we human beings not only communicate as we grow and age but also influences us as to how we think. The Chinese language is significantly different than English and this affects the very baseline of thought for native speakers. Chinese written language is all contextual, meaning that a single character can have multiple meanings depending on the context. A good example is the word Qi (氣) when found in writing about martial arts or Qigong it translates as energy, life energy, or the like. But when found in a weather report in a Chinese newspaper it is referring to air as in air quality. Context means everything.

When training or teaching Chinese martial arts, it is doing them a disservice to not investigate the poetry of the names of the movements and forms. A great deal of information is stored in these characters about the methods themselves. For example, the name of the basic stance Ma Bu (馬步) is commonly translated as Horse Stance and taught to young students by describing sitting on a horse's back. But investigating the context and characters used to describe the method we find that the second character is not stance but instead Step. It greatly changes how we should be thinking about the Ma Bu. It is not copying sitting on the back of a horse but rather describes the horse itself, powerful, immovable yet ready to move at any moment. It implies the potentiality of movement and not being seated and relaxed on the back of an animal. With this in mind, it is easy to see how more complex movements like Wild Horse Parts its Mane or Bear Exits the Cave (熊退出山洞) have many aspects of each movement contained in the poetry of the name of the method.

By taking your training to a place of deep understanding and investigation, many secrets of the arts reveal themselves. To be a teacher of others and take on the responsibility of passing on and keeping alive the skills it is worth the effort of finding deep understanding to help others. Each art has a great depth and breadth that gives it a beauty all its own. Taking on students is a responsibility that should not be taken lightly. Becoming the kind of teacher, you would want to follow is a good guideline when continuing your training as you accept students. While there are many ways to approach this, any profession will benefit from teachers of in-depth knowledge passing on their skills. We owe it to ourselves, our students, and our arts to drink deeply from the information found in them to pass them on in a way that respects their richness.

# Baguazhang: Taste the Tasteless

Ever made Congee? Take one cup of rice and ten cups of water and boil the rice until it explodes into basically mush. Then make it taste like something. Add chicken, mushrooms, tofu, soy sauce, chili oil etc. What is interesting about Congee is that it can be so many different types of meals. Chicken and mushrooms and chili oil are an entirely different soup than bok choy, black fungus and Hoisin sauce. It is the flavourless, Yin, basic Congee that is so boring that allows it to become so many tasty things. But no matter what is added to change its flavour, it never stops being Congee. Plain Congee is dull, but without it, we have no meal. Bagua is like learning to like plain old Congee, tasting tasteless.

Baguazhang has been one of the hardest and most rewarding arts I have practised. I love trying to unravel things, and reverse engineering an art built when all of the other internal arts were already around is more than difficult. Since Dong Haichuan created Bagua after Taiji, Xingyi, Xinyiliuhe, Xinyiba, and so on were already about, and the internal arts movement or evolution had already begun, he had access to a wealth of research and information on martial arts from which to draw. I am not going to go into the debate about whether Bagua is from Wudangshan or he created it himself there. Let's leave that by the wayside for now.

Dong also began by teaching people who were already masters of other arts like Cheng Ting Hua (Shuai Jiao) and Yin Fu (Shaolin Lohan). It would have played a significant role in how he approached Bagua to share it with them as opposed to teaching beginners in martial arts. Later in Dong's life, he did accept beginners as disciples, but there is evidence that he was not really the one teaching much at that point and it was likely Cheng Ting Hua teaching and building the drills for beginners during Dong's old age. Again, this is not the debate I want to wade in to here.

What was Dong trying to share with these students who had already accomplished high levels of martial skill? What is Bagua? Well, this is the question that has plagued me throughout my Bagua practice.

Baguazhang is the art of change, but what does that mean? In martial arts, we first train to understand and perform postures. We learn things like horse stance, black tiger stealing the heart, flash the back and so on. We prepare to link them together into choreographed sequences and practice them daily (ideally) until we can begin to apply these combinations on opponents. At first with partners in class, then non-cooperative sparring, we learn about the timing, distancing and power needed to implement these things. If we don't give in to the idea that we know better than our teachers by rejecting what we see as useless before we even understand it, we start to look at the meaningful use of these techniques. A decent player in any style should be able to apply the style they have learned by situation and circumstance with an opponent. Many times, this takes years. While lot of students never reach this ability due to a variety of reasons, some do and usually become teachers at this point. A few will get to the place that they are not even trying to apply movements to opponents anymore and instead will allow the opponent to put themselves into positions that resemble previous training methods and then apply them, letting the opponent decide what is used against them.

From the perspective of a beginner training to intermediate levels and trying to understand, Baguazhang does the same. Drills, forms, push hands, two-person work and forms, weapons, etc. are all practiced like any other art. By progressing into more advanced levels of training, we find all martial arts worth their weight focus on principles and mindsets to better understand the art itself and allow it to become more and more formless. What is meant by formlessness in martial arts? How do we achieve it? Why?

If we return to the idea of learning movements and postures and then linking them together, we can start to look at our training with a different mind. Yin and Yang theory (Taiji) is something given a lot of lip service in martial arts practice. While we understand it is something that should not be thrown away, we think of it as a way of thinking someone just gets. Applying the idea of Yin and Yang to training is of the utmost importance in developing a real understanding of your art. Yin and Yang are ways of defining aspects of a single thing to be able to understand its qualities better and to be able to examine parts of a whole. Without a distinction between this and that we are attempting to discuss the whole of the universe at once. It is far easier to break up things into their parts to better examine and understand them. Therefore, if we look at postures as snapshots in time during movements Horse breaks Free, Tiger descends the Mountain, and so on, we can define these moments as either Yin or Yang. Here I define postures as Yang, hard and apparent examples of martial arts.

They are the Obvious.

That means that between postures there are snapshots in time of Yin. Not-postures, moving and not static, the moves between the moves. As one of my masters said, "In between moves is the Gongfu." These moments of change and movement, the Yin in this case are where the real skill lies in training at this stage. It is not just superior structure and alignment in postures with names that is the martial art but the way we move from one to another without sacrificing all the necessary tenets of the art. In music, it is the spaces between the notes.

These Yin moments in training are the moments of change, the amorphous cloud where the player's body manifests power, structure, and skill then dissolve from that shape to create another one. Opponents do not fall from postures. They are defeated by movements. After some time, we start to see there are far more spaces between the movements than there are movements and postures themselves. Names of the postures begin to take on more and more meaning. They refer less to the appearance of the end shape. They apply more to the movement, mind, and spirit of the techniques. The Gongfu resides in the motion, not the stillness at its end. Horse breaks free from the corral is not about the punching posture at its end, but rather the charging, surging motion in the torso as though bursting through the timbers of a fence. The final strike need not even be with punches or even hands if the energy, intention, and mind come together correctly. Headbutt, elbow, who cares? If the purpose combatively is to kill the opponent, make him dead. It does not matter with what weapon.

Baguazhang has more moments in between than postures and positions by design. There are so few real postures in Bagua that they are almost manufactured for students to have something to latch on to when they are learning the art to make it less confusing. It is the motion and continuous rolling, coiling, surging, and twisting like a tornado that is the manifestation of the art. Bagua is movement guided by principles that run deep in the art like other truths, things like gravity, things that are real and proven to be true. I believe Master Dong found this in his training and when he began reaching past where his teachers of martial arts had taken him, he found this truth of change. Just as air density changes by altitude, yet remains air, Baguazhang is martial arts that changes regularly yet remains martial arts. The concept of change is not an idea to the Bagua player at high levels. It is an indisputable truth they are trying to embody through themselves.

There is history that says Dong did not initially even name his art Baguazhang. Instead, he called it Turning Palm or Changing Palm. Baguazhang was a name later adopted for it and most likely had to do with referencing elder Taoist concepts, as is the fashion with Chinese martial arts. There is also a legend that he only taught three palm changes to his students and worked with them on their strengths and backgrounds. He encouraged them to embody the principles and not worry about doing his art but instead doing their own. Looking at the arts passed down by his students we can see this clearly, Yin Fu Bagua is different from Cheng Ting Hua Bagua. They embody those men and how they trained, thought, and did martial arts. Again, "Do not seek to be like the men of old, instead, seek what they sought." Train the art with a teacher who can pass it on, work to understand it, and then allow it to change from your own experiences. The idea of doing something the same way for hundreds of years is ludicrous. Every master, student, teacher, and player does things differently according to their reality. If the principles of the art are kept intact, how is this change wrong? Master Dong Haichuan did not seem to think a change was a bad thing so why would we?

If you are starting reading this while starting your path into Baguazhang, do this. Study and practice diligently. Work hard to learn the movements and methods of your teacher. Train them until you can see the principles present themselves. Then work to be yourself in this life and allow your art to be a place of your expression of your understanding, love for the art, and authentic self. Let it be yours. As martial artists, we tend to always compare ourselves to the men of old in a way that makes them seem like supermen. We are the living art here and now, embrace that and find your happiness. Strive for perfection and be accepting and gentle with who you are. Baguazhang is a great art for this. Learn the form to become formless. You can't let something go until you have picked it up first.

# Demons Hands, Buddha's Heart.

鬼手佛心 - Gui Shou Fo Xin (Ghost/Demon, Hand, Buddha, Heart)

My right wrist bears this tattoo. The reason is different from what most people think. I get asked about it often, as it is my only obvious tattoo, and the reactions I get when I translate it are quiet, uncomfortable, and changes of subject. It's just like when I go to 'grown-up' dinner parties, and it's my turn to talk about what I do for a living. "Oh, you're an engineer? Cool. I pursue enlightenment through bare-fisted murder. More punch?"

So the conversation ends there, but I have had some people come back as they get to know me better and ask why I got the tat. Sometimes, it seems worth it to tell the story.

My second teacher-master in martial arts studies was Ma Qinglong from the Ma family style. When I started training with him, family systems were pretty much unheard of and honestly, I had never heard of them either. I thought I would check it out since I loved kung fu and was looking for a new teacher. Good or bad, it would be a new martial experience for me. On my first day, not only did I get to observe the students who would become my older brothers training things I thought only existed in movies or mainland China, but I got to feel them as well. I saw Drunken Boxing, Tiger sparring, Snake training, and the most insane workout I had ever been a part of, in the first hour! I was upfront with my new Shifu and told him about how long I had trained, where, and what, and all that jazz. I hoped that he would be alright with me not being a clean slate. Well, he looked at my nearly ten years of training and to judge, he made me spar. Not only was I completely taken apart with ease by the older students, but he would tell me to try harder, go faster, no worry, just fight. For those people who think kung fu schools never fight or spar, they never went down into the cave where Ma Qinglong taught. His rule was to fight twice as much as you train alone. I never left so much sweat and blood anywhere in my life than I did in the first months I trained with him.

Sounds ideal right? He was skilled, 'old skool,' and a fighter. Within my first week, he invited me back to his home after class to train and have a drink. His character then revealed itself more than it had before. He 'let' me 'spar' with him, not that there was a choice. Six or so beers in he wanted to see what I had and I felt the same way about him. We fought in his backyard under that damned old tree he made me work out under for years afterwards. I quite literally gave everything I had. I was the top student of my previous teacher, ran his classes, fought everyone, and it was the worst beating I had ever taken in my life up to that point. There were worse ones to come from him, but he was nice that night.

With every ounce of power and speed and skill I had, I attacked him over and over. He mocked and laughed at what I thought I had for power and told me to kick him in the torso as hard as I could, which I did, and nothing. It did not even take his eyes off me. He slammed my head through his white picket fence over and over knocking the boards out one after another. I know I went through it at least once back first as well from a throw of some kind. My memories are kind of blurry. I am sure I was not only too many drinks in but also concussed. When I woke up in the morning at home, I had blood under my nose and lips, a black eye that would last for weeks, and the worst headache of my life. My body was bruised up and I could even see where some of the more memorable strikes had hit me. I had never seen anyone who could drive their fingers into someone hard enough to leave finger marks before. It was a good thing there was not a class until after the weekend. Of course, that was a brief thought as the phone rang that day and he told me to get back to his house to fix his fence since I had broken it.

I ended up living with Shifu due to circumstances in my life, and he trained me. Unfortunately, it was almost always brutal. Learn to fall by being thrown. Learn to block by being hit. Fight every day. We had some good times too, of course. We would go out people watching and work on seeing their injuries and handedness and so on, applying the martial theory all the time. But even now twenty years later, when my Gongfu brothers and I get together, there is always release of some trauma caused by him. It was a shared experience for us, and we were all treated the same way. You either took it, or you quit, he did not care at all. Shug talks about the day Shifu broke his ankle, which I saw happen and Dom about having Shifu tear him open with his fingers. Seeing your blood spilt from someone just moving their hands across your flesh is a crazy thing.

So why the tattoo? Well, most people think it is to remind me to be gentle with my students and not be like my teacher. Keep the heart of the Buddha within and all that. But truthfully when I was on my own and teaching and training with other less severe teachers, I found myself so mentally injured by him that I swung too far the other way. I was not hard enough on my students. I never have and still never will allow myself to become him and treat people that way, but without some hardships in training, we lose many things. Some schools in Chinese martial arts don't even spar!

I became too soft on my students. The workouts got more comfortable and they sparred softer and softer. When I did techniques to them, it would be too gentle and kind. I knew what it was like to receive it much too hard and never wanted to put them through that. I worked to be compassionate and kind, but I was not doing them a service at all. Without eating bitter, we cannot taste sweet at all. I was not giving them enough bitter, and their skills were suffering because of it.

To balance ourselves and our lives, Yin and Yang, we must explore both sides. Without good killing hands you can't have profound healing hands and vice versa. Now I know some will debate this, but a surgeon has to be able to cut into people, carve pieces out, and be able to do so knowing that healing comes from it. Without the knife, no healing can take place. Without the bitterness of real training, no sweet can begin to taste.

So, the tattoo is my reminder, be balanced. Do not kill the students' skills with kindness. Nurture them with discomfort. Plant the garden of their Gongfu with some bitterness and toil. If the students never feel the teacher's real skills, they have no absorption of the reality of the art. Hiding it does no one any good. First, do not harm them. But be sure to let them know that you certainly could. Devils Hands, Buddha's Heart.

## Walking Home in the Rain

I once walked back to my place from my 18 Lohan Palm class, down the main street in Creston, in the rain. I saw the kids from the high school gathering at the local fast food for lunch, the lineup at Seven-Eleven for gas, and I passed so many people on the street that I knew. It was heartwarming. Small towns are beautiful in their way. There is a sense of comfort knowing many of the people you pass, where everything you need is, and how to get there. I felt this as I walked and listened to my music on my way home. I was thinking about the mornings lesson, about the true self (Hun) and the acquired-self (Shen), and how meditation in its many forms works to quiet the acquired-self so we can hear the whispers of our true selves, who we really are. The Lohan class was interested in these aspects of meditation practice and how strengthening our bodies help to enhance our minds and vice versa. I told the story of when I began my training in 1986 and my true self-seemed to scream in my ear that I had found my path.

As I neared my apartment downtown, I saw two young men approaching. One was displaying anger and violent intentions at the other who was trying to walk away. I saw the pushing and shoving as they neared me, and I took out my headphones to listen. They passed me. The violent one gave me a look meant to intimidate as I put my headphones away and looked down to show I expected not to confront him. When I turned heel and followed them, I was unnoticed as I was already out of his mind. Through the cursing and threats, I gathered money was owed, and the much larger violent man was going to beat it out of the other. Now don't get me wrong sometimes people need a swat in this life, be it by their mother's hand or the police, but I rarely feel it is appropriate for a larger opponent to beat and bully an obviously afraid and smaller one. When the first punch was thrown, I interrupted the impending beating with a "Hey!" This more massive, muscled guy turned on me, and his victim used the opportunity to run. My job was done. They can sort it out for themselves but not in front of me.

I was told to mind my business and keep walking. I responded with a simple agreement to keep walking, right towards him. He was right-handed, and so I moved towards his left shoulder to make him turn and have an opening for the side of my head. I looked at his face and let my body soften as I took my hands out of my jacket pockets and walked. Without any violence he allowed me to walk past him and comment on how I don't like seeing bullies, I don't like bullies at all. He stepped back to his right and into the puddle behind him. His wet foot and puzzled look were enough for me as I passed and continued home.

Sometimes I cannot mind my own business, but I realize that it is who I am. I made a promise to my teacher to help people in trouble if I could, and my true self cannot sit by and not do it. I had no desire to fight or teach him a lesson physically. But I was happy I was able to use my martial arts to help someone. Looking down at first took me away as a threat. It gave him false security and made him forget about me. Taking out my earphones allowed me to hear and decide what was going on and if anyone was with him as back up. Interrupting him after he became physical changed his attention and timing and allowed the other man to run. Pointing my intent at this left shoulder made him turn away from me and backup, making it only possible for his right hand to attack and his foot to step into the water, distracting him and, incidentally, giving me pleasure. Looking at his face and eyes let him see my lack of fear and hands coming out of my pockets as an intimidation tactic. Softening my body was to allow me to use my skills if I had to and conveyed predatory intent alongside my words.

It's so much more than kicking and punching. It comes to that sometimes, but there are so many opportunities to help others with what we learn and teach without violence. What annoyed me the most was that number of people on the street watching and trying to ignore the conflict. I understand not having the same skills to deal with it yourself but do something to help a fellow man, call the police, call for help. Don't just stand there. If you stand by and do nothing, eventually when you need to help others will do the same. It was an interesting morning.

# Fa Jing and Vibrating Palm

Both skills tend to be misunderstood. Most often, it is either being kept secret or not adequately taught to students or occasionally just referenced and whispered about as mythical skills from other masters or styles.

Fa Jin (sometimes Fa Jing due to pronunciation) is two characters. (發) means To Emit or Express. (勁) is a complex character that I prefer to translate as Whole Body Connected Intrinsic Power. The misunderstanding comes from the idea that there is only one type of Fa Jin which is considered an explosive type of movement. To express the whole body connected force does not mean only one type of force. Jins are like flavours of power. Each one is distinct and felt differently by the person touching the player. Famously Taiji people discuss eight jins in their art Peng, Lu, Ji, An, Cai, Kao, Zhou, Lieh but there many, many more. Examples include Han (Cold), Xuan (Dark), Pao (Fiery, Explosive), Zuan (Drilling, Boring) etc. Some of these express in an explosive way when demonstrated and these are the things people see when they observe players training. A common example of this shows up in Chen Taiji. However, this is not demonstrative of every Jin. Look to soft players like high-level Yang or Wu stylists, or Bagua players. The fact that they do not explode does not mean they are not expressing the whole body connected power. It is just not the type of Jin you can see.

The vibration or shaking seen in a player who is doing Fa Jin is a result of the body moving quickly into a solidly connected shape all at once. It is not the Jin itself nor is it representative of how the Jin is flavoured. It is an aftershock, a result of the power flowing through the shapes made by the body. Shapes are not power. Power flows through the shapes. So, this not Vibrating Jin.

Vibrating Palm is a famous method in Chinese Martial Arts that has a lot of mystery around it. This mystery coupled with secrecy and legendary storytelling is the cause of so much misunderstanding. Most likely it was founded in Tui Na (推拿) (translated as Push, Lift and Squeeze) which has a technique to release muscular tension through vibration.

Before Chinese Medicine was codified in about the year 1000, it was in separate parts among separate peoples. There were Acupuncturists, Herbalists, Bone Setters, Tui Na Massage, and An Mo Massage people. Sometimes there may be people who knew more than one method of healing but most likely they would be used individually or recommend patients to one another. You did not go to the Acupuncturist for the shoulder dislocation you got falling by the river. You went to the local Gongfu school since they were the ones who dealt with those types of injuries all the time. Many times, Tui Na was also the realm of the Acupuncturists and the Gongfu players since they had the grip strength to perform the massage methods well. Incidentally, An Mo massage which is the pleasant, relaxing type of massage as opposed to the therapeutic and awful feeling Tui Na was the realm of the blind, which gave them a way to support themselves after being trained.

The two types of Vibrating Palm training are internal and external. The external vibrating palm is used in Tui Na for massage and is a result of shaking the arm from the shoulder to create a vibration in the palm which you apply to the area you want to affect. In massage, it releases tension and feels excellent. It brings blood and attention (Qi) to the massaged area. The internal method most likely originated with martial artists who trained Tui Na. In the internal method, you train to begin the vibration for the palm in the Dantian and have it cascade in quick muscular contractions through the torso, shoulder, arm, and to the hand. The hand vibrates because the torso is transferring force through it, not as a result of shaking your hand. It takes time and effort (kung fu) to get it to start working at all.

So, we spend years training to vibrate the torso and carrying it through the hands. We set the palm on tabletops and shaking the table. We place palms on a wall and shaking the wall or post and so on. Perhaps you may find it from a master in a form you practice. I was lucky to be taught it in the Ma style of Gan Mao Quan, Sick Fist (感冒) and then find it again in Cao branch Yin Fu Bagua and Cheng Style Bagua forms. Once you have attained the skill and gained the internal ability to vibrate, what is its purpose?

Striking an opponent with the vibrating Jin is interesting. My Shifu was 'kind' enough to show it to me early on so I would get many chances to train it. Like cooking, it's best to taste the dish and know its flavour before trying to make it yourself. Powerfully done vibration Jin basically shakes the hell out of your structure and will cause it to open, weaken, or fall apart at its weakest point. I have experienced it and seen it done to others. A strike to the shoulder will buckle the knee or a strike to the chest would fold the hips, and so on. It also hurts like hell. It can affect organs as well, including the brain. In the Ma family training we focused on the skull or heart for ideally fatal results. But it works well in push hands as direction changes or in Qin Na methods to shake the structure and cloud the mind.
Fa Jin can be expressing different flavours, and one of those flavours is vibrating Jin.

# Eight Gates, Thirteen Postures & Jins (八門, 十三和勁)

Jin (勁) translates as Power. But this does not do justice to the character or the context in which we use it as martial artists. All Chinese characters are made up of what are called radicals. Each of these radicals has different purposes. Sometimes they imply meaning or origin of the concept and other times they suggest the sound of the pronunciation of the character. In Jin, we can see other martial arts concepts and characters as a part of its makeup. On the right of the character, we know the character Li (力) which means physical force, power, or physical strength. It is the drawing of an iron plough, something pulled by an ox. On the left side of the character, we have three other parts, the lower character Gong (工) and the upper parts of the character which we will get to after.

Gong (工) translates typically as work and can be combined with Li (力) to make the character Gong as in Gongfu (功夫). This is one of the monikers of the Chinese Martial Arts in general. To be specific, the character Gong (工) is a picture of a measuring tool, a carpenter's square. So now we have two parts of the character customarily translated as strength or power. One implying physical strength sometimes called Ox Power and the other the measured use of said strength. Intelligent strength is another way of translating this part of the character.

On the left side of the character are two more radicals. On the top is the character for the number one Yi (一), and the one in the middle is Chuan (巛) or river. Combined with the bottom left character Gong (工) they make up another character all themselves Jing (巠). Jing translates as a river flowing underground or something moving beneath the surface. When you look at all the parts of this complex character you start to see that the type of power, we are discussing is not just physical strength, nor something that can only be below the surface. It is a type of power that requires measurement, skill, intelligence, physicality, and training to manifest. Jin (勁) is, therefore, a more profound subject when talking about these subjects like the eight gates or eight jins of Taijiquan. When I teach my classes, I define the character as the whole Body Connected Intrinsic Power.

## Taijiquan Jin Shu (Tai Chi Power Technique) (太極拳勁術)

Peng, Lu, Ji, An are considered the four main jins of Taiji, and when the art is placed on a diagram like the Bagua, they take the cardinal directions of North, South, East and West. These are the jins that are supposed to be the first line of defense in the players' vocabulary for attack or riposte. They are the primary skills of the art, but it is a mistake to think of them as techniques. These jins are the principles and foundation of all the techniques of the art and are like the fuel that can pour into the engine of any method. These are the reason a movement found in Taiji and in Shaolin can look identical but feel so different when applied by a skilled player. Different jins mean different flavours.

## Peng (掤)

It is commonly translated as Ward Off but that tends to decrease student understanding. Peng is better translated as expanding the structure in all directions. It means that the structure of the player is paramount and must always be in alignment for the posture performed. And once the outer shape of the posture is correct, the Jin must also be present. It means expanding in all directions simultaneously from the core (Dantian). Allow every joint and every surface of the body to expand and realize its potential. If an opponent pushes against your Peng, he should feel as though he has no more effect than pushing against a tree. Inside your body, the sensation is expansive, and the mind imagines your presence filling up space. It is like filling a room as you enter the way a person of charisma does, like a rock star. The body expands and the mind's relationship to the space around the body changes and attempts to fill it. In old language this would be called expanding your Qi. Take up space with your body and mind during the manifestation of Peng.

## Lu (履)

The standard translation for this Jin is rollback, but this leaves much room for misinterpretation as well. A typical mistake I see in my students when they first learn rollback is that they tend to treat it as a retreat rather than a manifestation of a Jin. Lu is not running away from the force by changing the weight to the back leg. I prefer to translate this Jin as leading to emptiness, dissolving like smoke, or disappear. Lu is to deflect 1000lbs with 4 ounces. It uses the least amount of force to move the opponent's force away from doing damage to you. The old saying "The opponent's fist should brush your beard" would be an example of Lu Jin. Normally we see this labelled as sideways force to move an incoming power away from us, but that is too finite. It is leading the opponent to nothing, allowing their power to manifest uninterrupted but never allowing it to find its target. This is achieved by bumping the attack to the side or moving the body around it like a hand passes through incense smoke.

## Ji (擠)

Generally translated as press and matched with a technique with the hands touching one another. Directly translated, the character means to squeeze like crushing an orange for its juice. The idea of Ji Jin is to squeeze space around either your body, the opponent's body, or both. Using the example of the press movement in Yang style, we define a round, ball shaped area between the arms, the chest, and the palms. As we squeeze the area inwards with the elbows, the palms move forward as though the ball is changing shape. It gives us structure and motion equally. My preferred alternative way of seeing squeeze is to see a defined space in your structure during a shape; for instance, the area between your elbow and your knee in something like lazy about tying coat in Chen Taiji. If you place an opponent within that space and then move to squeeze that space closed with your structure, basic physics states that two objects cannot occupy the same space, so the one with the superior structure will remain. Most Taiji style grappling breaks the opponent's structure and use Ji Jin so the space they are standing in closes and pops them out of it. Owning the area within the body is structure and movement. Holding the space directly around the body sets up for Ji.

## An (按)

In Yang style, it is usually a part of the grasp bird's tail sequence (Ward Off, Rollback, Press, Push) and translated as a push. This is wrong. To push something away from your body is Tui (推), not An. But An, like many of these characters, is a word used in the context of martial arts differently than is generally seen in the language. An Jin is a type of force that harmonizes with the opponent's force and loads their body with your force simultaneously. In the Yang style sequence push would be better said as Push Downwards, Load and Release, Harmonize Downwards, or Receive, Deflect and Add, and Release. Harmonizing with an opponent's force is one of the secret words of Taiji. Take your opponent's pushing technique and push down on it and into their structure (legs). They will power upwards and forwards if they do not change methods and instead try to overpower you. Adding your downward force into their structure makes them add their force upwards, and when you release them, they bounce upwards and uproot themselves. It is like pushing a floating ball under the water and then removing all your force at once, so the ball floats upwards quickly, sometimes even leaving the water from the upwards force. Allowing the opponent to throw themselves is higher skill than overpowering them directly.

The four secondary Jins in Taiji [Cai (採), Lie (列), Zhou (肘) and Kao (靠)] are found on the Bagua diagram of the style in the four corners NW, NE, SW, SE and are meant to be secondary lines of defense when the art is in use. If one of the four primary methods does not work or your position is compromised, the four secondary ways are in place to recover your position and regain the tide of battle.

## Cai (採)

Cai translates as pull down but more accurately pluck like picking fruit from a tree. When picking fruit from a tree like cherries or apples, pulling down evenly or slowly will tear the stem and damage the fruit. In order to avoid this, we need a sharp and quick pull (plucking) of the fruit. The idea of plucking is used extensively by different martial arts including Taiji. The Cai Jin is meant to connect to the opponent's spine through the limb. The quick jerk steals the balance and ruins the structure making them vulnerable to another method or technique. Plucking is done on an angle rather than simply downwards, most effectively towards a hole or well in the opponent's stance. To easily understand the holes or wells in any basic stance draw a line between the heels. Ninety degrees from either side of this line will be the two main weaknesses in the stance and are the targets for effective Cai Jin.

## Lie (列)

Lie is a character meaning splitting or tearing force. When I explain this Jin to students, I use the metaphor of tearing a piece of cloth. Both hands must move in opposition to one another for the fabric to tear. This force of tearing or rending can be found all throughout Taiji practice with one limb or part of the body moving in one direction and its opposing portion balancing that action in the other direction. Basic physics "every action has an equal and opposite reaction" applies here. the issue in human practice is that we can disobey the equal force on both sides of the body rule. For example, in the Taiji movement walk backwards and ward off like a monkey we see the hands moving both forward and backward.

To have Lie Jin, other aspects of the body mechanics must be in play. The forward and backward arms must be equally drawing power away from each other originating at a single point. This is like pulling a string apart by pulling on each end evenly. The breaking point should be balanced in the middle. That is the point of origin of the split. This is not enough to call it Lie Jin. The parts of the body creating the forward and backwards movements of the hands must also be moving equally from one another. Another good example is in punching. It is not Lie if you merely push the fist forward. Split the length of the body by driving the rear leg into the ground and the fist forward equally, splitting the body in the middle. This is Lie.

An advanced form of Lie Jin, used when one can create it in their own body through practice, is being able to centre the point of origin of the tearing or splitting within an opponent's body. This is commonly seen in a basic arm breaking technique. The split begins in the joint of the elbow and reaches away in both directions, powered by our bodies taking the bones of the lower arm (radius and ulna) in one direction and the upper arm (humerus) in the other. Muscles, tendons, and other tissues are easily torn and damaged with this kind of force applied to them. At this level much of the force is spiraling.

## Zhou (肘)

This character means elbow. At first glance, it seems strange to isolate elbows or elbow techniques as having their own type of Jin. But when you consider the feeling that being struck with someone's elbow has, especially from a trained internal stylist, it becomes more apparent that there is a flavour to that type strike. To manifest internal force and drive it into another person's body we must generate that force via a cascade of muscular contraction. These are well trained nervous system responses to mind intent, proper alignment, and structure to deliver the power through the limbs to the opponent. The more joints the delivery of the power needs, the more chances there are for the structure and balance of the muscularity around the joint to be incorrect by leaking force or creating tangents of force that do not properly increase it. The correct use of the elbow as a weapon is effortless and powerful. because it removes joints from the system before providing the power. In Chen Taiji, for instance, it is common to see elbows resting on the torso and the torso twisted quickly (Fa Jin) to deliver the elbow into the target, removing all the joints in the arm and attaching the weapon directly to Dantian There is a Taiji saying "even the Masters fear the elbows of the youth."

## Kao (靠)

The last of the eight jins to discuss is Kao, translated most often as either Shoulder Body Bump or Body Attack. It is the ability to transfer force from your torso into the opponent directly and fiercely. The saying "Whole Body is a Fist" describes the idea here. Power can be delivered from any part at any time, which creates short-range power and opportunity to damage the opponent even in wrestling. The training for Kao Jin focuses on the back of the shoulders, sides of the shoulders and chest but Kao means any part of the body can be trained to deliver power. The shoulders are the easiest to accomplish while the rib cage and stomach are more difficult. The lower back, top of the head, and hips are most difficult. The training is often dissimilar from other Taiji exercises so is often not associated with the style by many people. Iron body methods that involve bumping into walls, trees, or other players work on the ability to deliver force out of the different parts of the body. Exercises like Xinyiliuhe Body Banging Carp jumps out of the Water, Bagua Bear rubs Back, and others train this. Any part of the body can train in this way by bumping incoming force from any angle. Kao is a powerful tool for rescue when the opponent has passed through your four primary jins.

## Ting (聽)

The above eight jins or eight gates are not only present in the form and combat but in the intermediary of push hands where we train with a partner. Without the ability to touch and taste or hear the jins it is difficult if not impossible to gain a real understanding of them. From a Yang style perspective, we see the primary four jins worked in the Peng, Lu, Ji, An sequence of push hands the most commonly seen drill. It is important to feel and change the Jins as the movements progress and not to contest with your partner too early. Studying through touch supports the discovery of another of the jins of Taiji Ting Jin (聽勁) or listening energy. It is not listening with the ears but reaching out with your sense of touch into the partner or opponent to feel their body as it changes. Listening in this way gives you the ability to feel a movement begin earlier, like feeling the spine turn before the hand moves or the abdomen begin to turn before the spine. Training with a partner lets you feel them move and manifest the jins and this sensory input allows you to learn to recreate that feeling in your own body. What people now call Disciples were once called students Allowed to touch the Master and feel him change and use the jins to pick them up directly from the source.

The second set of push hands exercises known as Da Lu or four corners push hands is meant to work the secondary jins of Kao, Lie, Zhou and Cai with a partner in the same way.

## The Five Steps (Bu 步)

It is the eight Jin and these five steps that make up the 13 postures. The five steps are Jin, Tui, Ku, Pan & Zhong Ding. In the simplest terms, these translate as step forward, retreat backwards, look left, gaze right, and central equilibrium. These are all found in the forms of Taiji and are also all found in the Yang style movement grasp bird's tail. Each section of grasp bird's tail associates with one of the steps. Looking, gazing and central equilibrium are especially important. Looking is predatory and is focusing on an opponent directly, moving your intent towards them and carefully studying them. Gazing is the vision of a prey animal, watching and gazing towards the horizon looking for predators. It is a soft vision that uses the peripheral to see around the opponent and softly gazing into them. Looking and Gazing is much like Ting Jin (Listening Energy), both focused and unfocused, predatory and watchful, aware, receptive and ready. Without training the eyes the intelligence of the body is useless.

Beyond theses postures, the following quote from Mike Sigman is useful in seeing the differences between Yang and Chen Taiji.

Note the differences between the Chen and Yang styles for the five steps. The Chen style: Teng: Sudden upward-angles strike (Yang: step forward), Shan: Sudden emptying downward (retreat); Zhe: Bend/close opponents arm back on him (look left); Kong: Sudden emptying not quite downward (Gaze Right); and Huo: Overall smooth and flowing (central equilibrium).

## Zhong Ding (中定) Stand like a balance, turn like a wheel.

Central equilibrium is the ability to find verticality in the body which relies on the spine and skeleton as well as axial force. The central pole of the body must be like a vertical axle, unmoving from side to side but able to rotate at will. It receives the power and turns it away from the spine and creates the force at the same time. The whole of Taiji revolves around the ability to have Zhong ding. It is one of the reasons structure is of such importance in Taiji training.

## Four Secret Words

While the 13 Postures are the more common words used in Taiji training, there are others including the following Four Secret Words. Few people teach them and almost never openly. These words represent high level push hands methods. You need to work through the first methods as a base to build the more difficult skills of Mi, Kai, Dui, and Tun. I only touch on them here. "It takes three lifetimes to learn Taijiquan."

Mi - Spread Qi over the body and the opponent
Kai - Lightly cover
Dui - Equalization of force
Tun - Drink the power

## The First Moment

First, you should only use your martial arts in the direst of circumstances where you cannot verbally avoid or physically run away, no matter how skilled you are. Fighting always leads to someone being hurt, usually both parties. This injury can be catastrophic and life-altering or it can just be having to live with yourself for harming another human being. Even in the case of being so skilled that you did not need to harm the enemy badly to control the situation, there is still the mental anguish of having been thoroughly controlled physically or having to deal with doing that to someone else. There is always damage when combat takes place.

But we practice for when it is absolutely necessary. Fights are most often won or lost in the first moments of the confrontation. The Chinese saying is that a fight should last three heartbeats, no longer. It is a time frame of only a second or two, and while it may seem like a myth, this is what they mean. Fights begin the moment it can no longer be avoided. The first moment when you both know it is about to take place is when everything begins. It is when hands start to rise to guard positions, legs begin to flex and stabilize the body, and the mind decides that violence is necessary. That is the first moment of combat and it is often ignored in martial arts training.

It is in part due to the modern way of looking at fighting and fight sports. In any competition, from full contact MMA to Point sparring in a local tournament, it was decided decades ago to make sure that neither person started with an advantage. Fighters begin at a safe distance from one another with a referee telling them to prepare. When both are set, a command to begin is given. The entire first moment where fights are won or lost has been sanitized to create a fair and safe environment for competition. It makes good sense, it is not life or death in these matches. But it affects the way everyone trains and thinks about violent confrontation. We believe this is the norm since it is the way the 'professionals' do it, as we see on TV. But let's take a step back and look at fighting in the past for a moment.

Unless a formal challenge match was taking place, things were not fair. They were not meant to be. Ambush was and is the most effective way to destroy an enemy. Attacking from behind, in the dark, silently, without their foreknowledge is the easiest way to win. Yes, it is dirty or Guerrilla tactics, but it is the reality and has worked from time immemorial. The Biaozhi or Chinese Bodyguard company members would escort people or merchant trains from one city or town to the next to protect them from being attacked by bandits. Banditry is a lucrative profession, especially when there is little to no policing or government interference. In an excellent solid ambush, everyone dies, and the bandits get the cargo. The Biaozhi were ready to take on these ambushes during the journey. So why is it that an ambush is so effective? It is simply lack of preparation. Letting your enemy get adequately prepared for battle makes no sense unless you are engaging in some form of ritualized combat. Seize the initiative, and the opponent must try and recover it, which is usually the beginning of the end for them.

## Seizing the Initiative

Seize control of the first moment. That is the smartest way to ensure you have the earliest advantage. If you allow an enemy to put up their defenses and find their balance, you are merely missing the opportunity to win. The Gongfu family method I teach uses "If you're not Cheating, you're not trying hard enough" as a motto. Find every advantage and take it for yourself. If the opponent begins to pick up his hands, attack him. Steal his balance, batter his body and head, and make his defenses a heartbeat slower than your attack. Use your martial arts to secure control of the fight from the first moment and never give the initiative back to them. It is why I teach methods of entering the opponent's defenses. Once you have the eight methods of Beat, Cross, Sleeve Release, Dragon, Tiger, Snake, Horse, and Shadow, we work on making them faster and closer to the start of the opponent picking up their hands until at full speed you can seize initiative instantly. The rest of the fight is up to your training. A grappler will take them to the ground and work from that advantage. A striker will try to hit as hard and as many times as possible once they have initiative. In the case of something like Traditional Chinese Martial Arts, they will try to kill the opponent as quickly as possible. Yes, I know it sounds brutal but training this way changes everything in your martial arts. It is easier to decide not to kill an opponent than it is to try and go through with it.

> "In times of war, a prolonged battle does
> harm to both sides."
> Sun Tzu: Art of War

## Life & Death in the Palm of Your Hands

For many, this is the reason for beginning Martial Arts Training. There are writings citing about exercise, self-confidence, and self-defense as reasons to train, but there is a dark underbelly to the martial arts that draws a significant number of people. That is the power to hold someone's life in your hands.

While all the above reasons are a great impetus to start a career in training martial arts, few people are willing to accept the part of them that is a predator and can kill another. Some will argue that Martial Arts are all about peace and harmony, not murder, but we must understand that by acknowledging the peace and harmony side of the arts we must recognize its opposite. Humans have evolved as predatory omnivores. Our binocular vision is a result of needing to calculate distances to prey for hunting and our teeth are both suited for the eating of plants and flesh. To deny this fact about our evolution is to stunt our own ability to grow, change, and study who we really are. When it comes to martial interaction with others in our species, we also must acknowledge that our fighting methods come from a place and time where life and death hung in the balance.

Those drawn to the training for the ability to wound others have encountered their dark side and found it gives them a type of power, a feeling that is easy to think of as self-confidence or self-assuredness. However, they are often masking feelings of inadequacy under the persona of this Dark Passenger. While some genuinely need help and do not have accepted standards of mental operations, this is not about mental health. I am addressing those who fall into the training for the feeling of power it can present to them. It is time to recognize these people exists but often ignored or left to their own devices.

In the old days of martial arts training, a Master would have few students, but even the most popular, powerful teachers in an area would still have many requirements before letting their disciples learn the secrets of their arts. I have spoken to and trained with a few Masters of the old school mentality. It is apparent that secrets are kept today. I have trained under a Master for close to ten years before closed-door sessions would take place, knowledge being passed on with warnings.

"Do not teach this to white people."
"You teach this, you teach only special students."

These and other such were experiences come directly from my life. I have always been an inquisitive type and the reason that was given is to protect society. Giving real martial arts to people with poor character is and was considered a sin. The students who irresponsibly used their Masters' teachings on others reflected directly back at their teachers. The tradition of Taking back the art, which is to break both the student's collarbones, is the punishment for this misuse. In a different age, it was not uncommon for a student to die if necessary.

So, what was being kept a secret? It is the most effective techniques, ways of thinking, and training that will make an art come to life. If the Master did not trust the character of the student, Wu De (Martial Virtue) would prevent these things from ever being shown unless the student radically changed who they were. In today's age, it seems that martial arts secrets are just fairy tales and do not exist. You can go on YouTube and see great masters doing any art. But the truth is that sometimes something as simple as a single sentence can change someone's martial understandings forever and allow their skill to blossom. These students who are not willing to stay long enough with their teachers, or willing to change how they think and act through training, never know these things exist. That is why they are considered fairy tales. Unfortunately, the majority train for a few years and go off to become teachers themselves, never receiving the transmission from their teachers. It's not their fault they started teaching. They did not know there was more to learn.

That is one of the problems with secrecy in martial arts. If something is genuinely kept a secret the student never trains or changes themselves as necessary to learn it. They do not know there is something expected of them or that there is something more to learn from their Master. Styles die like this. Masters pass away without having shared everything. Students become teachers only because they were around at all the right events for long enough, so they MUST know what they are doing. It is how many Arts become the emaciated corpses we see today. No real meat is left, just the husk of something formerly tremendous and powerful.

Secrecy does keep things out of the hands of thugs, but some Masters are too worried and will not pass them on to anyone, even after years of dedication. This type of Master most often falls back on the axiom of protecting the style, not society. The style needs to stay secret, or others will have it. Other people will know what they know, and they think bringing others level up to their own is not empowering but instead takes away their own greatness. So, there are Masters not passing on what they know and killing their arts.

## Brothers in Arms

When I was a kid, I fell in love with G.I. JOE, the cartoons, the comics, and the action figures. Yes, old-school G.I. JOE was my thing, especially the Ninjas. Snake Eyes and Storm Shadow, the coolest names for ninjas ever, Ever, were part of a fantastic and heartfelt story. Both were training brothers under the same Master, and through those years they became family. True brothers are chosen and not just blood. As life went on, they chose different paths and ended up on either side of the conflict between COBRA and the Joe's.

In the BEST G.I. JOE comic ever, The Silent Issue, the two masked ninjas combat. At the end, it is revealed they are brothers, displaying the same tattoo on their forearms. The story continued through subsequent issues and my young heart hung on every word and image. The idea of going through hardships with someone making a strong bond between you spoke to me. It still does. Gongfu Brothers are for life. Your brother will help you move. Your Gongfu brother will help you move a body.

Respect for our teachers and their importance on our path should never be overlooked for a minute. Something we forget is the essential parts our Gongfu Siblings play in our training. It is just as important as the role of our Masters, only different. Without my Gongfu brothers I never would have made it to where I am. I would never have kept going to class when things were rough. I would not have been able to cry, bleed, or rant the way I needed. I have many brothers. I have received a gift in Dominic, Daniel, Kevin, Jason, Lorne, but here, I want to write about my brother Shug.

When we met in 1995, I honestly thought he was more than a bit strange. He was like everyone who trained with Master Ma, but even more so. He was last to finish every workout, never hurrying up to get to the good stuff. What a weirdo, I thought. Every push up was correct. Every punch was hard, fast, and accurate. Each was slow enough to be correct but fast enough I would not want to be in the way. Shug started training with Master Ma when I was still with Chin Woo, eight years my senior. I was lucky enough to be paired with him now and then when something needed to be careful. He taught me our sticking hands. Every day for months we would work together, and he would explain carefully and demonstrate things repeatedly, slowly, so I could get it. Every time I was frustrated or tired of it, I would try and speed up and test things out. Every time it was met with a gentle, slow palm on my chest or face that was never seen or stopped. His point abundantly clear. So many nights Shug would drive me home in his crappy Camaro, and we would sit for hours talking about training. He would show me techniques in the car or outside in the snow. We would rant about Shifu and compare bruises, and he would patiently try to answer all my questions, night after night. He would always remind me slowest is fastest during training, take your time and understand, don't rush.

Shug had started martial arts the same year I did but he began with a Taiji master while I was at the Chin Woo. So, by the time I started Taiji training he had already been training internals alongside with our shared master for nearly ten years. Even though I went to other teachers to learn, I always came back to Shug to test, talk and debate. When I started training under the now well-known Chen Zhonghua, it was Shug that helped me work out the kinks, make sense of the things I learned and test my techniques. By 2006 Shug had been training Yang and Chen Taiji for 20 years and Ma family Gongfu for 18 years. His insights were gold, and because we loved each other, he never held anything back. When I began training with Master Chen Qi Ming in 18 Lohan Palm, Shug took over teaching my Sunday classes, so I could spend each Sunday with Shifu. The first time I showed him the Lohan, his words were "That's not for beginners now is it?" He encouraged me never to let it go. Years later, I am Shifu's disciple and see him every chance I get.

Shug lost his sight when he was in his early 30's from a condition known as Retinal Detachment. Legally blind, he still kept up his training. His sticking and pushing hands have become so much more refined since then that I started joking with him about being the Blind Master (Snake Eyes & Storm Shadows training brother). Shug had his first heart attack when we were pushing hands on a Sunday morning. Luckily, I had learned a bit of Chinese Medicine from Shifu Chen, and I was able to needle him and calm things down before we took him to hospital. He has had seven heart attacks since.

The last time I visited him in the hospital, they were telling him he should have a defibrillator surgically implanted in his heart. It was a most intense conversation we had about Tao, life and death, and about why he was choosing not to have it done. He told me that accepting and not fearing when your time has come is Taiji. It is Tao. He went home and the next day he was walking his dog Jasper as usual. He pushed hands with me and visited my school when he could to be Uncle Shug my students. He gave them tastes of what it was like training under our teacher. Every time he would have a new test for me and my practice and homework for me while he was gone.

One summer I went to Edmonton to visit everyone, and Shug arrived late at the Gongfu-BBQ. Even though he was tired and had been working all day, he pushed, stuck, and trained with every one of my students who were there. At the end of the night, we pushed hands by the firelight and whispered to one another. We laughed and tried tricks on each other and talked and pushed. It was not really about the training anymore, but about being family.

Without him, my martial arts would not be anywhere near where they are now, nor would my love of them be as strong. Without being able to sound things off him from my other teachers, I would have been struggling to understand much more often. Has he been more important than my Masters? No. Is he as important? Absolutely.

Don't forego your training partners, your martial family, for anyone. They will bleed with you and for you if you will stand by them. Training is not all about skills and fame and breaking things with your hands. It's about the path you walk and the people who walk it with you.

# The Bear & Eagle Fight for Survival (熊和鷹的戰鬥中生存)

For the name of a martial arts form, that is pretty damn cool. When I started learning the names of movements and forms in Chinese martial arts all it did was make me think it was even cooler and more mystical than I first thought. to quote my Gongfu brother Kevin Walbridge, it is the "exotic otherness" that attracts us from the west to the Asian martial arts in the first place. We are drawn to the ability to look awesome, dress in old style clothes, burn incense, and pretend we are in a Shaw Brothers movie.

The trappings of the art may have brought you to it and helped you stay interested during hard times, but you start to realize those trappings have real meanings and learning them changes the way you think and train. They begin to increase your understanding and can affect how well you perform techniques and forms. Most of the poetry and metaphors in martial arts seem so foreign to us they are hard to understand. Phrases like Bear and Eagle Fight for Survival or Wind Sweeps the Cobblestones seem only flowery at first but taking the time to decipher them can change everything.

Most of the old names have to do with everyday tasks or views one would see. That way a student would see swallow skims the water in their mind and make the connection to the method they are learning. But speaking a different language in a different time makes all this more difficult to understand.

Bear & Eagle Fight for Survival is a form taught in the Xinyi Liuhe Quan, Heart/Mind Six Harmonies Style (心意六合拳). We know there are ten animals in the style and the first two moves in one of the forms are Bear exits the Cave and Eagle flies through the Forest. What does it imply to our practice of this set? And if you are not a Xinyi player why should you even keep reading?

One of the many profound connecting principles in the martial arts is the concept of Yin and Yang reversal. All things transform, are always in motion, and are always progressing towards their seeming opposite. At a workshop I was teaching none of the participants, all with more than 15 years of training and many teachings and running their own schools, had any real understanding of Yin and Yang. Martial arts teachers and 'masters' that could not explain Yin and Yang at any more than a grade school level or how it applied to the techniques we were practicing, or their arts made me kind of angry, sad and disappointed.

Yin and Yang is a relationship, defined by opposing forces, a continuum. Nothing is Yin or Yang in and of itself. The two opposites define one another such as the ideas of day and night. Without day there would be no night nor any name to call it or reason for a title. But they are not two separate things. They are two sides of the same coin. In either microcosm or macrocosm, the entire universe is defined by Yin and Yang. Males and Females are merely humans on different parts of the continuum. It is not black and white but a range of understanding interrelated opposites. To know the light, you must know the dark, and vice versa. For instance, with Taijiquan, you cannot only study the health and get the full understanding of the art. Without an in-depth knowledge of the combative side, you cannot gain the full health benefits, since you only know a small part of it. Also, the Ji (極) refers to the moment of transformation from Yin to Yang or vice versa. Ji is the moment where a motion, upwards for example, reaches its extreme and stops to become downwards. The very name of the art is about the study of Yin and Yang and its constant state of transformation. Taiji is NOT a Great Ultimate Super Magic Martial Art of the Ancient Chinese Immortals.

Bear and Eagle represent Yin as closing the body and Yang as opening the body. Contracting and expanding take place move after moving throughout the set in Xinyi. Bear exits the cave closes the body while eagle flies through the forest opens the body from. It is a constant study of the transformation of Yin and Yang, and so they fight for survival. They are continually transforming into one another, born and dying over and over throughout your practice. Understand this and you practice the set in a way that was not apparent before, the areas and times of opening and closing. Knowing the posture or shape of the movement is not enough. If the movement is supposed to open, then what does that mean? How does the body open and expand and stretch? Are you doing those things or just making shapes? Every opening has a closing and vice versa. Where are these taking place? For example, in Bear exits the cave the shoulders round and close, the chest softens, the legs crouch. All the while the fingers open and expand, showing the Yang within Yin. Every movement does this. And not just in Xinyi Liuhe Quan either!

A deeper understanding of the culture, language, philosophy, and thinking of the people who originated the art you study will drastically change the quality of your martial arts. I have seen it take place in myself and others. So many times, I have also viewed the result of going to class a couple of times a week for so many years that you get promoted to a teaching rank and still understand nothing. The arts are only alive because of the people right now, today who are preserving them. Are you going to pass on a corpse or a living breathing thing to the next generation?

> "I have heard that in ancient times there were the so-called Spiritual Beings;
> They stood between Heaven and Earth, connecting the Universe;
> They understood and were able to control both Yin and Yang, the two fundamental principles of nature;
> They inhaled the vital essence of life;
> They remained unmoving in their spirit;
> Their muscles and flesh were as one -
> It is the Tao, the Way you are looking for."

The Yellow Emperor's Classic of Internal Medicine
(Huang Ti Nei Ching)

Like any quote from ancient texts, this can be interpreted in many ways. The difficulty of studying ancient books is that it always comes down to our perspective when reading it. This passage does have some implications for us as martial artists, Qigong players, and people doing self-work. Standing between

Heaven and Earth is how I tend to describe human beings during my classes. That is the beginning of finding vertical in the body. The ability to stand in such a way that the spine and skeletal system transfer most of the weight through the body to the earth is something we all need to practice for structural and combative reasons. The Taiji classics mention this type of training and every master I have trained with begins with this as a fundamental to the art. Releasing the tension of the body that usually suspends the weight in the musculature allows those muscle groups to relax and increases their ability to do work. Stand Tall like the Monkey, The Taiji Ridgepole, The Iron Rod are names I have heard from teachers working on this state with their students. While none of this is new information to most Taiji players, there is another layer that seems to be discussed rarely.

The discussion of Yin and Yang is overdone and in often simplistic with little thought to the depth of the principle. Most people training can discuss the equal oppositions, that context means everything, and probably quote some medical or philosophical texts on the matter. Putting the principles into practice must be the top priority and quoting the famous is not the same as understanding it for yourself. For instance, to stand between heaven and earth, we need to understand the interplay of the opposites genuinely to create relaxation. Studying the interaction in our bodies is a way to directly experience this profound principle. That is why I train. Discussing the universe is great over tea or in college dorm rooms over bongs but studying it inside your own body, part of the world like everyone's, is another matter. How do we stand between heaven and earth? To reach the top of the head towards heaven first, I need to press my feet down into the ground, effectively going down to go up. Reaching up with the head creates downward sensation in the body and increases the pressure on the feet. The two opposites are changing and complementing one another.

Standing practices of Qigong work this a great deal, standing still, unmoving. It seems to me that most of the issues I see with people's skills have to do with skipping over these things that seem too 'simple' to train. We never know what the hell we are being taught until much later. The best-skilled people I have met go back to basics, see the importance of learning to stand, sit, walk and turn as the basis of their art. The ability to stand with a level of true relaxation (Song) allows us to learn to move in that state and ideally to fight in it as well. Taiji is not about focusing on winning and losing. In combat, it is about allowing the Yin-yang interchange to continue in your body and between the two of you.

Tightening up and thoughts of 'winning' or 'losing' are a departure from the present moment and an attempt to stop the interchange of Yin and Yang. This is not the way the universe works. It's going to change whether you let it or not so Taiji is a way to learn to deal with that. I know when I get out of my own way and just let things change without fighting them, my life is a lot easier. This is fighting without fighting.

The great principle of the interchange of Yin and Yang (Taiji) is a lot to digest. Go down to go up. Press the foot back to create force forward. Do not try to be strong, just be strong. It is very Yoda. Integrate your mind into your flesh, allow them as Yin and Yang to work together like heaven and earth. There is no "I" controlling my body. I am my body. If you cannot get past thinking that mind and body are separate how are you ever going to deal with the idea that an opponent and you are one? When we study Yin and Yang, we are examining the entire universe while we are part of it. We start studying ourselves, our training methods, forms, postures, and breathing exercises. But we cannot lose sight of the fact that they are work, meaningful, challenging, frustrating work. The more I get entrenched in it, the more there is to unravel, more than a lifetime's work that's for sure.

The most straightforward stuff is the hardest. The first lessons are the most advanced. Focusing on goals distract you from the present work so just do it. To quote my teacher, "shut up and train."

# Be Like Steam

When I asked Master to look over my Xinyi Liuhe and Baguazhang, he agreed and stepped back for me to perform. As I settled my stance and my nerves, he sat down at the tea table and picked up his cup. His eyes never left me. I started carefully going through the Lao San Zhang, the three old palms of Cheng Baguazhang, first. After walking a couple of circles and running the palm changes, I stopped and switched to Xinyiliuhe Bear Exits the Cave posture.

Master sipped his tea and although his posture seemed casual, his eyes were like a tiger never leaving its chosen prey. I started to do the Bear and Eagle fight for survival form from Xinyiliuhe. As always, I enjoyed the explosive, relaxed movements. Turn and chop in Dragon Body felt good and the crack of it tearing through Chicken Head Shape was satisfying. After Iron Bar and Suicide on a Tombstone I stopped and waited to hear what he had to say, doing my best to control my breathing.

"Three levels to a trained body in Bagua," he remarked. "The first body like a snake, connected and strong. Second body like water, heavy and relaxed. Your body is like water." I was fairly pleased that I was not at the lowest level in his eyes as he continued, "Third body is like a Tornado, like steam rising from a pot, like a snowstorm. Bagua is like trying to fight a snowstorm. You will always be surrounded."

He gave me some exercises and advice on my Bagua, getting up from his chair and demonstrating. He fixed my postures and let my touch and feel him move. We did applications and I touched his feet to feel the spirals originating there. It was not long after that lesson I started tearing my shoes during practice.

"To the opponent, you are like a storm, everywhere at once. To you, he is like snow falling while you are talking to a pretty girl.

by Sifu Neil Ripski

You are never distracted from the girl. You don't even feel the snow. They are nothing, cannot distract you."

When I first challenged him years earlier, he told me my body was intelligent and like water. When I asked how he beat me so quickly, he replied: "I am like steam!" A half-decade after that Bagua lesson, I finally started to understand what he meant by steam. Having no other distractions in my life while I travelled in Nepal and India allowed me a lot of focus on my morning training. My mistake at first was thinking that the steam reference was like heat or fiery, flowing movement. But it is about removing more and more of the self from the equation. The question "Who is doing Bagua?" is becoming more and more in the forefront of my mind and the answer keeps leading me to release more and more.

Water, even hot water is heavy and dangerous, but it can be contained in the vessel it is heated in. Steam is free of even the vessel itself. Bagua is amazing and difficult.

# Dantian is a Prison (叛徒太極氏族)

"What if Dantian is a prison?" my Gongfu brother asked me years ago. I was shocked at his words. "What the hell does that mean?"

I thought he asked me to think about it for a while as was his way in everything. So I did.

Over the years we had many, many discussions, tests, and debates on this and many other subjects that sprang from it. It was the beginning of me starting to get somewhere on the internal side of training. It was rebellious, outside the box thinking from what our teachers had taught us. We both trained under Master Ma but had different Taiji and Qigong teachers from different lineages. It was the beginning of the Renegade Taiji Sect (叛徒太極氏族) and the beginning of some real progress for us.

What if Dantian is a prison? It is.

It is a prison of thought and belief. Dantian represents a belief system that limits and idealizes a particular way of thinking and looking at the body and the arts. It venerates one specific lineage in most cases. Dantian in internal martial arts practice is an essential stage of training and has to be carefully attended. It creates the origin point of movement and allows cascades of muscular contraction to take place from the centre of the body, rippling out the extremities. That is an absolute necessity for internal power and real connectivity in the flesh. But that does not mean it is the end of the training. It is only a stage.

When students start training in martial arts, they are purely external since it is the human condition. Then, using imagery and metaphor, they begin to become internal. The idea of Dantian is a method for them to accomplish the internal journey. However, it becomes a prison when one insists it is the only method and refuses to move from this stage of training to another. The cascade effect from this training remains important, but the use of the mind only on this effect in practice does not allow for growth to other methods. Changing the way we think about exercise, about the body, about our art is how we grow and change. That is the way all the arts tell us we should be.

If Dantian is a prison, then what changes if we look outside the box? If the body always moves from the core without the need for conscious thought continually directing it, then the mind is free to pursue other things. In styles like Taiji and Bagua, it is the skills we use without having to try that we have mastered. As an example, in demonstrations of Iron-Body there tends to be a dramatic build-up of breathing and esoteric looking hand movements. This may be fine for demonstration but if the person needs a minute or even thirty seconds to prepare to do Iron-Body then that skill is still not useful in combat. There, it needs to be completely unconscious, automatic, and natural. All our skills we are working on must become like this. Peng Jin (expansion power), Song Jin (relaxation/accepting power), Iron-Body, etc. all need to be merely a part of us. Dantian moves first is one of these skills that must become a part of us entirely as well.

When my brother and I were testing our theories and ideas on each other. We tried to move past our old ways of thinking and training, so we had a few rules.

One: Anything we dream up, we must test on each other without the knowledge of the other person. If they can stop it unconsciously, then it is not likely worth pursuing.

Two: When something works it must be taught to the other person to see if it can be transmitted and replicated. Skills that are not teachable may be useful to the person but not the art.

Three: Touch and test with every single person you can find. Ask questions and seek out Masters for help and bring that information back to share.

I think the martial arts are in our hands and hearts, not in the hands of the long-dead famous names in the styles. They are alive right now, right here in us, the players of today. If we want to move forward with our skills, we always need to push the boundaries, not just wait for a Master to show us something new. If you want to try something, try it, but test it out and see what comes of it. Your Master will tell you if it's a bad idea and most likely it will result in an excellent chance for him to teach you something new. What is the meaning of Traditional anyway? I say it is "Trying to advance yourself and your art in every possible way." The arts should not be museum pieces, left stagnant under glass. They should be evolving and alive. Use everything you can bring to make them better in the long run.

The Renegade Sect needs more members.

# Parting Shots

by Sifu Neil Ripski

The project to get this book together has been a long process of more than three years. I am already working on the Special edition of the Secrets of Drunken Boxing Series with additional information on the Eight Immortals and how to use them in the style and training. Even though it seems like I always have more to do, at least it is a labour I love. My life has changed a lot since I started this book. I find myself in an entirely different place. Divorced, travelling and teaching all over the world, and sharing what I can with everyone. Hopefully, I am helping them along their way.

I must say many thanks to my teachers and Gongfu brothers without whose help I would not have a single thing to say about martial arts. Thank you all so much.

Thank you as well to the WUMA (World United Martial Arts Association) Nepal Branch and Master Animesh specifically. He made my teaching in Nepal happen and so much fun that I cannot wait to go back. Master Udip, Drunken Master in Nepal, thank you for sharing your time with me, it was a pleasure to check out each other's styles and see how we are indeed of the same martial family of methods.

Warren, my brother, my friend, and my student at times, without him these books would not be in print at all. His patience and huge heart have helped me accomplish so many things in this life already. I owe him a debt of friendship and so much gratitude. Thanks, brother, Abide.

Sami, one of my Eldest students and a Drunken Master in his own right has always been around for me try an experiment on, lay hands on. His fantastic eye for detail martially, and in editing has made my blathering readable. If anyone ever gets a chance to train with him, it is well worth it. There are only a few Masters like him.

To You, reading this. Thank you. Without people interested in my works and Drunken boxing, in general, the style I have will die. We who live and train now are the lineage holders of these arts that give us so much. Thank you for helping to keep it alive!

"Don't look back. You're not headed there."

by Sifu Neil Ripski

THE END

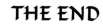